The Search for the Northwest Passage

Jill Foran

WEIGL PUBLISHERS INC.

Published by Weigl Publishers Inc.
350 5th Avenue, Suite 3304, PMB 6G
New York, NY 10118-0069

Web site: www.weigl.com

All of the Internet URLs given in the book were valid at the time of publication. However, due to
the dynamic nature of the Internet, some addresses may have changed, or sites may have ceased to
exist since publication. While the author and publisher regret any inconvenience this may cause
readers, no responsibility for any such changes can be accepted by either the author or the publisher.

Library of Congress Cataloging-in-Publication Data
Foran, Jill.
  The search for the Northwest Passage / Jill Foran.
     p. cm. -- (Great journeys)
  Includes index.
  ISBN 1-59036-205-5 (library binding : alk. paper) — ISBN 1-59036-259-4 (pbk.)
  1. Northwest Passage--Discovery and exploration--Juvenile literature. 2. Arctic regions--Discovery
and exploration--Juvenile literature. I. Title. II. Great journeys (Weigl Publishers)
  G640.F67 2005
  910'.9163'27--dc22

                                    2004002875
                     Printed in the United States of America
                     1 2 3 4 5 6 7 8 9 0   09 08 07 06 05 04

Project Coordinator
Donald Wells
Substantive Editor
Tina Schwartzenberger
Copy Editor
Janice L. Redlin
Photo Researcher
Andrea Harvey
Design & Layout
Bryan Pezzi

Credits
Every reasonable effort has been made to trace ownership and to obtain
permission to reprint copyright material. The publishers would be pleased to have
any errors or omissions brought to their attention so that they may be corrected
in subsequent printings.

Cover: Arctic icebergs (Photos.com); **Daryl Benson/Masterfile:** page 7; **Corel
Corporation:** pages 3, 5T, 5B, 16, 17L, 26; **John Foster/Masterfile:** page 25;
Glenbow Archives: pages 18 (NA-694-1), 19 (NA-1512-1), 29 (NA-694-1; NA-1512-
1); **Bryan Pezzi:** pages 12, 13; **Photos.com:** pages 1, 4, 6, 8, 10, 11, 14, 15, 17R, 21,
22, 23L, 23R, 24, 27R, 29; **James P. Rowan:** page 20; **Galen
Rowell/CORBIS/MAGMA:** page 9; **Jim Steinhart:** page 27L.

**On the Cover: Icebergs are a hazard to ships sailing through
the Northwest Passage.**

Contents

The Long Search

The Northwest Passage is a sea route. It links the Atlantic and Pacific oceans. It runs through Canada's maze of Arctic islands. The passage lies between Canada and Greenland. It is about 500 miles (805 kilometers) north of the Arctic Circle and only 1,200 miles (1,931 km) from the North Pole. It is a difficult route. It is plagued by countless icebergs, biting winds, and freezing temperatures. These conditions prevented European explorers from discovering the existence of the Northwest Passage until well into the nineteenth century.

In the late fifteenth century, it was believed that a northern passage would provide a new shipping route from Europe to Asia. For the next four centuries, bold explorers set out to find and complete this passage. They struggled through the **labyrinth** of Arctic islands and channels. They failed, time and again, to find a northwest passage. Despite all the failed **expeditions** and tragedies, many explorers did not give up in their search. They faced starvation and disease to find the mysterious passage. Sadly, many of them died in their quest.

The existence of a northwest passage was proved in the 1850s by Robert McClure. It was many years, however, before anyone was able to sail the entire passage. This journey was first completed between 1903 and 1906 by the Norwegian explorer Roald Amundsen.

Fascinating Fact
It is known today that there is more than one Northwest Passage. The melting and shifting ice in the Arctic regularly creates or blocks passages.

Navigational equipment such as this antique compass helped early explorers search for the Northwest Passage.

The Unforgiving North

Wildlife and extreme weather conditions are some obstacles that northern explorers must overcome.

Early explorers to the Arctic discovered a harsh environment. The Arctic was filled with icebergs, brutal winds, narrow straits, winding channels, and many islands. The biggest challenge was the ice. Explorers soon learned that the sea in the far North froze over for most of the year. Sometimes the ice trapped the explorers' ships. In some cases, it crushed ships. The luckier expeditions waited out the winter and continued exploring after the ice melted. Winters in the Arctic are dark and frigid. Temperatures often fall to -50° Fahrenheit (-46° Celsius). The winds never cease. The Sun barely shines. Early explorers trapped in the Arctic during the winter usually suffered greatly.

Winter temperatures average -27.4° Fahrenheit (-33° Celsius) in the Arctic.

The Lure of Untold Riches

The desire for wealth and riches inspired the search for the Northwest Passage. Italian explorer John Cabot knew that England wanted to find a new sea route that would lead to China's gold, silk, and spices. The eastern routes around Africa to Asia were long and difficult. Worse, they were blocked by Spanish or Portuguese warships. In the late 1490s, Cabot convinced King Henry VII of England to pay for an expedition to the northern regions of the Americas. Cabot knew the world was bigger than Christopher Columbus claimed. He told King Henry that Columbus had not sailed far enough to reach Asia. He believed he could find a shorter, more direct passage to Asia across the top of North America.

Cabot did not find the route to Asia. However, the idea of a Northwest Passage to easy riches persisted. Beginning in the early sixteenth century, many European countries sent explorers to find this direct passage to Asia. As they searched for this route, early explorers managed to map much of North America. However, they could not find the fabled Northwest Passage. The search for a northern shipping route was not abandoned. In 1745, the British House of Commons offered a £20,000 reward—millions of dollars in today's money—to whoever found the passage.

Fascinating Fact
Pepper was more valuable than gold in eleventh-century Europe.

The Riches of Cathay

In the early days of exploration, Europeans called China "Cathay." This was a medieval name. It was made popular in the 1300s by the writings of Italian explorer Marco Polo. For centuries, Europeans read stories and descriptions of Cathay. Many of these writings described the wealth of this mysterious country. From these stories, Europeans came to believe that Cathay was a land of untold riches. Therefore, the desire to gain access to this wealth and establish trade with Cathay and other parts of Asia was strong. In the fifteenth century, the southern routes to Asia were mapped and controlled by Spain and Portugal. By the early 1500s, both countries were bringing back riches, such as pepper, through these southern routes.

The Chinese junk is one of the strongest, most seaworthy ships ever built.

Ship Shape

With the exception of a few **overland** treks, the search for the Northwest Passage took place in ships. Over the course of 400 years, the style and size of these ships varied greatly. In the early years of the quest, explorers used whatever ship was available and affordable. Many of these ships were considered **sophisticated** for their time. They often were not suitable for the harsh, ice-laden waters of the North. Still, many of these ships managed to withstand the harsh environment and heavy beating of the North Atlantic waves for more than one journey. In the 1600s, the sturdy 55-ton (50-metric tonne) *Discovery* was used for six voyages to the North.

Gradually, ships sent to the North became more powerful and reliable. Wooden ships were strengthened to make them seaworthy for Arctic sailing. **Hulls** were reinforced with a second layer of oak planking. The **bows** of the vessels were **sheathed** in metal. This helped them butt their way through sheet ice. For example, the Norwegian ship *Fram*—which means "forward" in Norwegian—was built in 1892 to withstand Arctic ice. The *Fram* had a triple oak/greenwood hull that was 24 to 28 inches (61–71 centimeters) thick. It could proceed under steam or sail power. The *Fram* was so sturdy it was able to make two trips to the Arctic and one trip to the Antarctic.

Samuel Hearne was the first European to walk from Hudson Bay to the Arctic Ocean.

Navigating the North

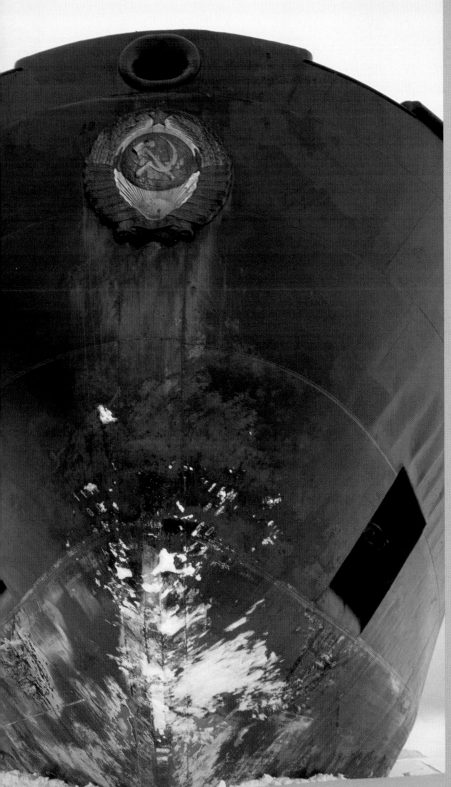

Early explorers did not have the luxury of using radio, radar, and computers to calculate the position of their ships. Among the early **navigation** tools used by Arctic explorers were the cross-staff and the back-staff. The cross-staff was first used in the early 1400s to determine a ship's latitude, or position north or south of the equator. First, a sailor would use the cross-staff to find the **altitude** of the stars, Moon, or Sun. From this measurement, navigators could find their ship's latitude. In the late 1500s, English explorer John Davis (also spelled Davys) invented the back-staff to determine a ship's latitude. Davis's back-staff was a welcome invention because it allowed sailors to stand with their backs to the Sun while taking measurements.

Enormous ice-breaking ships help explorers reach uncharted areas of the Arctic.

Hopeless Race to Riches

Beginning in the sixteenth century, several European countries were anxious to find a northern passage to Asia. These countries included France, England, and Holland. In the 1520s and 1530s, France sent explorers such as Giovanni de Verrazano and Jacques Cartier to find a route to Asia through North America. In the early 1600s, Holland's Dutch East India Company sponsored expeditions to find a northern passage on behalf of Dutch merchants. Everyone wanted to have control over this passage.

The English were the most persistent explorers in search of the Northwest Passage. In the 1570s, England sent Martin Frobisher and John Davis to the Far North on different expeditions. These two men managed to explore as far as Baffin Bay and the Davis Strait. In the 1610s and 1620s, there were more efforts by English explorers. These expeditions were frustrating. Early explorers encountered blocked channels, dead ends, and freezing weather. They learned that the Arctic had a harsh environment that was difficult for Europeans to endure. These voyages proved to England and other countries that the Northwest Passage through the Arctic might exist. However, it would not be an easy or fast trade route. Hopes for an easy trade route across the top of North America to Asian riches faded.

Fascinating Fact
While many explorers were searching for the Northwest Passage, others searched for the Northeast Passage to Asia. The Northeast Passage was thought to run north of Scandinavia, into the Arctic Basin, and along the north coast of Asia.

The British East Indies Company was formed in 1600 to conduct trade in Asia. The company ruled India from the mid-1700s to 1858.

In recent years, large pieces of Arctic ice have broken apart and started to melt. Less ice may make it easier to travel through the Northwest Passage.

The Merchant Adventurers

England's merchants played a large role in initiating early expeditions to the North. English merchants wanted to find foreign markets for their goods, especially their cloth. They believed that one of the best markets for their goods would be in Asia. In December 1553, a group of London merchants formed the Merchant Adventurers, or the Company of Merchant Adventurers of England for the Discovery of Lands Unknown. This company was established to pay for voyages of exploration. The Merchant Adventurers raised enough money to buy and equip three ships. These ships were to be used for a voyage to Asia. The Merchant Adventurers decided to attempt a northeast route to Asia instead of a northwest route. Their expedition failed to reach Asia.

Arctic Maps

Some scientists think that **global warming** will open the Northwest Passage to cruise ships, tankers, and warships within 50 years. The route through the Northwest Passage from Europe to the Far East is 2,485 miles (4,000 km) shorter than the route through the Panama Canal. Some people have started to refer to the Northwest Passage as the Panama Canal North.

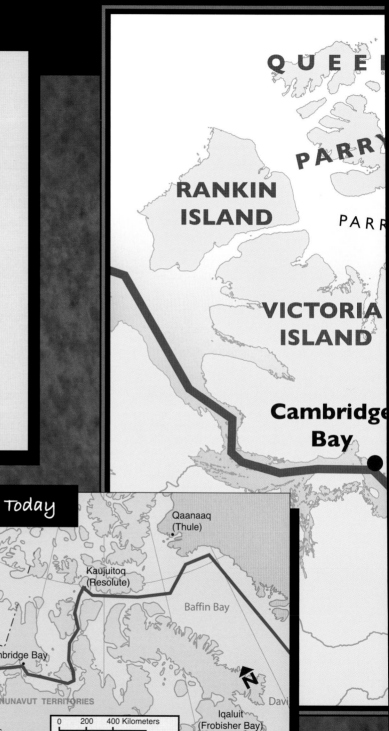

QUEE

PARRY

PARR

RANKIN ISLAND

VICTORIA ISLAND

Cambridge Bay

The Arctic Today

Prudhoe Bay

U.S.

Beaufort Sea

Qaanaaq (Thule)

Fairbanks

rage

Dawson

Inuvik

Kaujuitoq (Resolute)

Baffin Bay

YUKON TERRITORY

Whitehorse

Mackenzie River

Echo Bay

Cambridge Bay

Great Bear Lake

NUNAVUT TERRITORIES

eau

Watson Lake

NORTHWEST TERRITORIES

Iqaluit (Frobisher Bay)

Davi

BRITISH COLUMBIA

Yellowknife

Great Slave Lake

Fort Nelson

Hay River

Fort Smith

Kangiqcliniq (Rankin Inlet)

Ivujivik

Prince Rupert

0	200	400 Kilometers
0	200	400 Miles

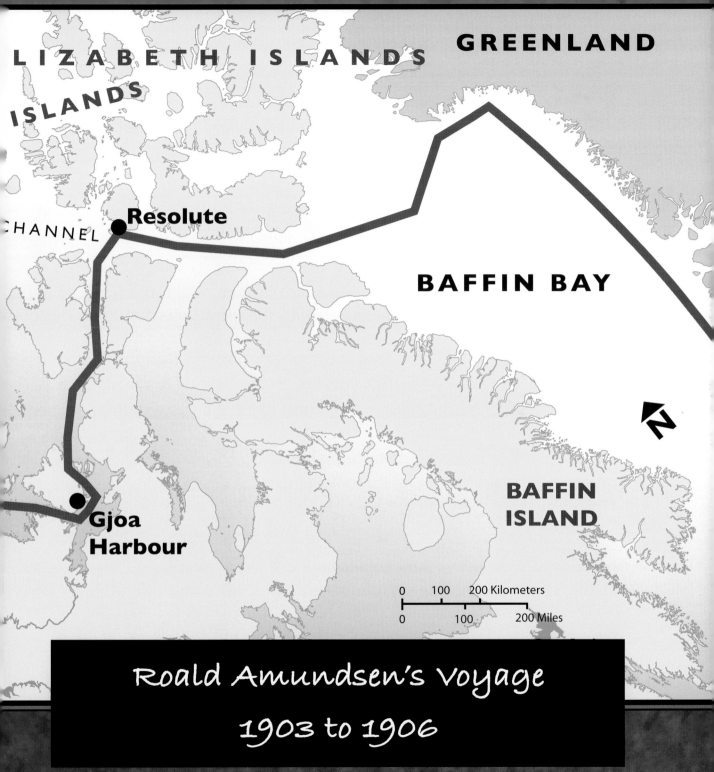

LIZABETH ISLANDS

ISLANDS

GREENLAND

CHANNEL

Resolute

BAFFIN BAY

BAFFIN ISLAND

Gjoa Harbour

0   100   200 Kilometers

0   100   200 Miles

Roald Amundsen's Voyage 1903 to 1906

Unexpected Encounters

Europeans were not the first people to explore the Arctic. The Inuit had lived in the vast region for more than 1,000 years before the arrival of European explorers. The Inuit were **nomadic** people who had learned to survive in one of the coldest places on Earth. Until the sixteenth century, they had no contact with Europeans. They knew little about the world beyond their region. Similarly, early explorers knew nothing about the Inuit. However, over the next few hundred years, many northern explorers and groups of Inuit encountered one another.

Sometimes these encounters were filled with violence and tragedy. The Europeans and the Inuit did not always know what to expect from each other. This could lead to disagreements or battles. One such battle occurred in 1612. That year, explorer Thomas Button and his men tried to **commandeer** canoes from some Inuit. A fight broke out. Five of Button's men were killed.

Friendships also developed between the Inuit and the explorers. In 1585, John Davis and his crew made friends with several Inuit. They entertained the Inuit with music and gave them gifts. Other European explorers had similar experiences. The Inuit supplied explorers with valuable information about the uncharted coast. They also showed the Europeans how to stay alive in the harsh environment. The Inuit taught European explorers how to hunt for caribou, fish for seals, and prevent frostbite.

The Inuit wore masks as a way of praying that there were many animals to hunt.

Mutiny!

Inukshuk are stone figures that the Inuit use as hunting and navigational aids.

The long search for the Northwest Passage is filled with cases of murder and **mutiny**. One of the most famous cases took place during Henry Hudson's fourth and final journey to search for the Northwest Passage. In 1610, Hudson and his crew left England and headed north. From the beginning of the journey, some members of the crew were unhappy. There were threats of mutiny. By November, the ship was frozen in ice. When the ship was finally free of the ice, Hudson decided to continue the expedition. The majority of the crew did not like this decision. They forced Hudson, his son, and several sick and loyal sailors into a small boat and then headed for home. Hudson and the others were never heard from again.

Fascinating Fact
Until the latter part of the eighteenth century, warfare between Europeans and the Inuit made southern Labrador and the Strait of Belle Isle—both located in what is now known as Canada—a dangerous place.

Finding the Northwest Passage

Early explorers quickly learned that the Northwest Passage would not be an easy trade route. However, eighteenth-century explorers continued to search the Arctic for a northern trade route. Explorers such as Samuel Hearne and Alexander Mackenzie searched for the passage on foot. They walked thousands of miles across the Canadian North. Some of the expeditions in the 1700s yielded useful and interesting information about the passage. However, wars between England and France in the early 1800s put the search for the Northwest Passage on hold.

Fascinating Fact
In 1912, Norwegian explorer Knud Rasmussen became the first European to complete the Northwest Passage by dogsled.

By 1818, the wars had ended. England once again turned its attention to the Arctic. This time, the English were not searching for a road to riches. Instead, explorations were made in the interest of science. The people of England wanted the mysterious north filled in on their maps. Between 1818 and 1847, many sea and overland expeditions were launched to map the Arctic. The Franklin expedition was one of the most famous sea expeditions. John Franklin and a crew of 134 men left England in 1845. Sadly, the entire expedition disappeared in the North and was never seen again. In the following years, more than sixty-five expeditions were sent out to search for these missing men. On one of these expeditions in the 1850s, Robert McClure proved a Northwest Passage existed. He traveled from the Atlantic Ocean to the Pacific Ocean by ship and by dogsled.

The Mackenzie River in Canada is named after the explorer Alexander Mackenzie.

Dogsleds enabled explorers and hunters to enter hard-to-reach areas as well as carry large loads of supplies.

Scurvy

Early Arctic explorers did not have access to the fresh fruits and vegetables that contain vitamin C and other essential nutrients. As a result, many sailors contracted scurvy, a disease caused by a lack of vitamin C in the diet. In most cases, their skin turned black, their teeth fell out, and their gums bled. They suffered from ulcers and had difficulty breathing. A number of explorers died from scurvy. For many years, no one knew what caused scurvy. In 1747, a naval surgeon, James Lind, prescribed lemons and oranges as a cure for scurvy. In 1795, the British navy distributed lime juice during long sea voyages. This is the reason British sailors came to be known as *limeys*. Some Arctic explorers learned from the Inuit that whale blubber would prevent scurvy.

Famous Arctic Explorers

Martin Frobisher (1539–1594)

Martin Frobisher was one of the first explorers to search for the Northwest Passage. Frobisher was 14 years old when he went to sea for the first time. He became a well-known navigator and explorer. He was also a pirate who brought many treasures back to England and Queen Elizabeth I.

On June 7, 1576, Frobisher embarked on his first journey to the Arctic. With two ships and a crew of thirty-five men, he sailed north and landed near Resolution Island. He named this island "Queen Elizabeth's Forelande." He then sailed to the eastern tip of Hall Island and claimed the land in the queen's name. From there, he found a waterway he believed was the Northwest Passage. He named this waterway "Frobisher's Streights." Although he did not reach Asia, he returned to England with items from the North. One item was black rock, which he claimed contained gold.

In 1577, Frobisher was sent to the North for a second time. He returned from his second voyage with 200 tons (181 metric tonnes) of the black rock. He was sent back in 1578 to set up a colony and mine 2,000 tons (1,814 metric tonnes) of the black rock. Frobisher and his crew returned to England without finding any precious metals, such as gold. Soon after, it was discovered that the black rock he had found on his first voyage was worthless iron pyrite, or fool's gold. Despite this, Frobisher's journeys fueled further interest in exploring the North.

John Ross (1777–1856)

John Ross was born in Scotland in 1777. He learned his navigation skills on merchant ships. After **apprenticing**, he served with the British navy in the Napoleonic Wars (1803–1815). Following the end of the wars, the British Admiralty assigned Ross to lead an expedition into Davis Strait and Baffin Bay to search for the Northwest Passage. In April 1818, Ross left London with two ships. After reaching Davis Strait, he proceeded to Lancaster Sound. There, Ross became convinced he could see mountains in the distance and that the way was blocked. His crew thought he was wrong, but he decided to return to England. Ross's hasty decision tarnished his reputation. It was proven 1 year later that there were no mountains blocking Lancaster Sound. Ross had seen a **mirage**.

In 1829, Ross made another journey in search of the Northwest Passage. Ross sailed beyond Lancaster Sound and then south into Prince Regent Inlet. There, the ship got caught in ice. The crew was forced to spend the next 4 years in the Arctic. They were the first explorers to survive that long in the Arctic. During these years, Ross and his crew explored parts of the Arctic on foot. They collected scientific **specimens**. Ross's nephew, James Clark Ross, mapped the location of the **Magnetic North Pole**.

In 1833, Ross and his crew were rescued by a whaling ship and returned to England as heroes. Ross received thousands of letters congratulating him on his survival skills.

S ailors who ventured into the Arctic to find the Northwest Passage did not have it easy. They endured long voyages, often spending years at sea. These voyages were filled with danger, hardship, and hard work. Sailors toiled almost constantly while on board a ship. They performed their daily tasks in terrible winds and freezing temperatures. Sailors had many daily tasks. They watched for icebergs and land. They cleaned the decks. They cared for the sails. Their sleeping quarters were cramped and dirty. Their main food staples were beer, biscuits, and salted meat.

Fascinating Fact
Sailors did not own watches, so time was kept by ringing a bell.

Ice was the largest obstacle faced by early Arctic explorers. The sailors had a very short season in which they could actually sail on the Arctic waters. From late autumn to late spring, the northern waters were completely frozen. However, by July, the ice would begin to break apart into jagged **floes**. It was then that the sailors could continue their exploration. Still, the waters were never completely clear of ice floes. This meant explorers had to ease their ships through very narrow channels created by the floes. Often, they had to tow their ships around the floes. Ships sometimes took days or even weeks to travel a few miles. Sailors had to do their best to fight their frustration.

Christopher Columbus was searching for a western water passage to Asia when he landed on the Caribbean Islands in 1492.

Christopher Columbus's Crew

Some people believe that Columbus's crew on the first voyage to the Americas were criminals. This is not true. They were nearly all experienced seamen. It is true that the Spanish monarchs offered freedom to any convict who signed up for the voyage. However, only four convicts accepted the offer. One convict had killed a man in a fight. The other three were his friends who had helped him escape from jail. On the first voyage, the eighty-seven crewmen on the *Niña*, *Pinta*, and *Santa Maria* were paid between $12,509 and $25,018 U.S. in today's money. Masters and pilots were paid $50 to $200 U.S. per month. Able seamen were paid $50 to $100 U.S. per month. Ordinary seamen were paid $33 to $66 U.S. per month.

Sea ice in the Arctic has been melting rapidly over the past 3 decades.

The First European through the Northwest Passage

The Northwest Passage was proven to exist in the 1850s. It was another 50 years before a ship actually sailed through it. The man who sailed through the Northwest Passage was Roald Amundsen, an explorer from Norway. In 1903, Amundsen and six companions set sail on a small fishing boat called the *Gjoa*. By 1906, the crew had steered east to west through the passage. Amundsen kept an account of his journey. In it, he explains how his crew spotted a ship in the Pacific Ocean and knew they had successfully completed their journey.

The Pacific Ocean's name comes from the Spanish word *pacifico*, which means "peaceful."

At 8 a.m. my watch was finished and I turned in. When I had been asleep some time, I became conscious of a rushing to and fro on deck. Clearly there was something the matter, and I felt a bit annoyed that they should go on like that for the matter of a bear or a seal. It must be something of the kind, surely. But then Lieutenant Hansen came rushing down into the cabin and called out the ever memorable words: "Vessel in sight, sir!" He bolted again immediately and I was alone.

The North West Passage had been accomplished—my dream from childhood. This very moment it was fulfilled. I had a peculiar sensation in my throat; I was somewhat overworked and tired, and I suppose it was weakness on my part, but I could feel tears coming to my eyes. "Vessel in sight!" The words were magical.

Shortly after Roald Amundsen navigated the Northwest Passage, his ship was frozen into the ice. It remained in the ice all winter.

Modern Exploration

Since Roald Amundsen's successful journey through the Northwest Passage in the early 1900s, other explorers have continued to challenge the North's icy waters. In 1942, Royal Canadian Mounted Police Sergeant Henry Larsen became the second man to sail through the Northwest Passage. He and his crew sailed from Vancouver, British Columbia, to Halifax, Nova Scotia. It took Larsen and his crew 28 months to travel over the top of North America. They sailed in a **schooner** called the *St. Roch*. In 1944, Larsen turned the *St. Roch* around and completed the Northwest Passage from east to west in 86 days.

Both Amundsen and Larsen used relatively small vessels to navigate the Northwest Passage. However, later twentieth-century explorers began to tackle the passage in more powerful ships called icebreakers. In 1954, a 6,500-ton (5,900-metric tonne) Canadian icebreaker called the *Labrador* plowed through the passage in only 68 days. Over the next few years, other icebreakers continued to chart new northern routes. In 1969, a group of oil companies spent $40 million to equip an enormous oil tanker called the *Manhattan* with a powerful engine and a special ice-breaking bow. It was seventeen times larger than any ship to sail through the passage. The enormous oil tanker made the trip in record time. However, it suffered serious damage. Once again, plans to use the passage for profit were abandoned.

Fascinating Fact
In 1960, the United States Navy nuclear submarine *Sea Dragon* pioneered another northwest passage by traveling under the polar ice.

Oil companies wanted to use the Northwest Passage to transport oil from Alaska to Philadelphia.

The Icebreaker

Icebreakers are heavy ships designed to break the thick ice in Arctic and Antarctic waters. Modern icebreakers are made of steel. They have a double hull and a rounded bow. The rounded bow enables an icebreaker to rise on top of the ice. This allows the ship's weight to break through ice much like a sledgehammer breaks through cement. Russian and American icebreakers are able to break through ice 6 to 7 feet (1.8–2.1 m) thick.

Icebreakers are very expensive to build and operate. They are also uncomfortable to ride in—breaking through the ice causes constant vibration and noise. Still, these powerful boats have made it possible to sail through polar waters with greater ease and fewer tragedies.

Icebreakers shoot hot water at Arctic ice through jets located just below the water line.

Lasting Effects

For centuries, the long, difficult search for the Northwest Passage was a popular subject among Europeans. The public listened to the tales of explorers who had braved the North and survived. Many explorers wrote books about their Arctic adventures. Early artists created paintings and drawings of the Arctic based on explorers' stories. Today, the history and present state of the Northwest Passage fascinate many people. Songs, books, and films about the passage are still produced. Also, new types of exploration are being conducted in the Arctic. For example, the Mars Society is a group preparing people to travel to Mars. This group is conducting experiments and testing equipment on Devon Island in the Canadian Arctic. Devon Island is one of the most Mars-like environments on Earth.

Fascinating Fact
Since 1906, only 60 ships have traveled the entire length of the Northwest Passage.

The Northwest Passage is not considered a good shipping route because of ice. However, many scientists claim that the Arctic **icecap** is slowly melting. According to these scientists, global warming has already begun to slowly melt the icecap over the North. It is possible that in just a few decades global warming will have melted enough of the ice to open the Northwest Passage for shipping, tourism, and fishing, at least for part of the year. Such a possibility would have been a dream come true 400 years ago.

Devon Island is located in Nunavut. It is the largest uninhabited island in the world.

Arctic Sovereignty

The northern lands around the Northwest Passage belong to Canada. Canadian officials consider the waters of the passage internal waters. This means they believe that non-Canadian vessels must request permission to pass. However, the United States and other countries do not accept Canada's claim to **sovereignty** over the waters of the Northwest Passage. In 1969 and 1985, the United States sent oil tankers into Canada's Arctic without permission. The United States argued that it had a right to send the tankers because Arctic waters are not internationally recognized as belonging to Canada. In 1988, Canada and the United States reached an agreement that allowed U.S. icebreakers access to Arctic waters on a case-by-case basis.

Submarines allow scientists to explore areas that are hard to reach in the Northwest Passage.

Northwest Passage Time Line

1497 to 1498
John Cabot claims Newfoundland for England.

1534 to 1542
French explorer Jacques Cartier surveys the coast of Canada and the St. Lawrence River and searches for the Northwest Passage.

1576 to 1578
Martin Frobisher makes three voyages to the North and reaches Baffin Island and Frobisher Bay.

1585 to 1587
John Davis commands three voyages in an attempt to find the Northwest Passage. He makes a correct guess about the location of the entrance to the passage.

1609 to 1611
Henry Hudson explores North America's east coast and sails on the river and bay that now bear his name.

1818 to 1833
John Ross embarks on three expeditions to the Arctic. On the second expedition, Ross and his men are trapped in the Arctic for 4 years.

1845
John Franklin leads an expedition by sea in search of the Northwest Passage. Officers and crew are trapped by ice off King William Island. The entire crew is dead by 1848.

1850 to 1854
Robert McClure penetrates the Pacific entrance to the Northwest Passage and completes the passage partly by ship and partly by dogsled.

1903 to 1906
Roald Amundsen successfully navigates the Northwest Passage by ship.

1942
Sergeant Henry Larsen becomes the second man to sail through the Northwest Passage. He is the first to travel from west to east.

1944
Sergeant Henry Larsen completes the Northwest Passage from east to west in a single season.

1969
The oil tanker *Manhattan* sails the Northwest Passage in less than a month.

The four-century search for the Northwest Passage was filled with excitement, adventure, and tragedy. Many explorers were admired and celebrated for the expeditions they led into the Far North. Others were shamed for their failures. Still others died on their quests. Below are the names of ten men who devoted much of their lives to finding the Northwest Passage. Choose one explorer, and research his journey to the Arctic. Once you have learned all about his northern voyage(s), imagine you are one of the crew members on the expedition. Write a long journal entry or letter to a loved one that describes the explorer and the journey he is leading.

Martin Frobisher	John Ross
John Davis	William Parry
William Baffin	John Franklin
Robert Bylot	Robert McClure
Henry Hudson	Roald Amundsen

1. Who was the first explorer to complete the Northwest Passage?

2. What disease plagued many sailors during their quest to find the Northwest Passage?

3. Which Arctic explorer saw mountains blocking a passage through Lancaster Sound?

4. Name two navigational instruments used by sailors.

5. Whose lost expedition caused explorers after him to chart much of the unknown Arctic?

6. Why was the Northwest Passage important?

7. Who first explored North America's Arctic regions?

8. Who found fool's gold while searching for the Northwest Passage?

9. What is the biggest obstacle in Arctic waters?

10. Name the first boat to navigate through the Northwest Passage.

Answers on page 32.

Web sites
www.allthingsarctic.com
This site contains profiles of several important Arctic explorers as well as fascinating facts about the Arctic and the search for the Northwest Passage.

www.nlc-bnc.ca/2/24/index-e.html
This site presents a history of the search for the Northwest Passage century by century.

Books
Blashfield, Jean F. *Cartier: Jacques Cartier in Search of the Northwest Passage*. Minneapolis: Compass Point Books, 2002.

Warrick, Karen Clemens. *The Perilous Search for the Fabled Northwest Passage in American History*. Berkeley Heights, NJ: Enslow, 2004.

altitude: the height of something above a particular specified level, especially above sea level or Earth's surface

apprenticing: learning a trade or skill

bow: the forward part of a ship

commandeer: to seize another's property for public or military use

expeditions: journeys or voyages that are made for a specific purpose, such as exploration

floes: sheets of floating ice

global warming: an increase in Earth's atmospheric temperature, causing changes in the climate and environment

hulls: the bodies or frames of ships

icecap: a thick cover of ice over an area

labyrinth: a maze of paths or passages

Magnetic North Pole: the spot on Earth to which the north moves a little bit each year

mirage: a misleading appearance of something in the distance; an illusion

mutiny: a rebellion against legal authority, especially by soldiers or sailors refusing to obey orders and, often, attacking their officers

navigation: the science of getting ships, aircraft, or spacecraft from place to place

nomadic: moving from place to place, with no permanent home

overland: proceeding over or across land

schooner: a fast sailing ship with at least two masts and with its sails parallel to the length of the ship rather than across it

sheathed: covered

sophisticated: complicated or complex

sovereignty: having power or authority over a region

specimens: typical examples of animals, plants, and minerals

Answers to Quiz on Page 30
1. Robert McClure 2. scurvy 3. John Ross 4. the cross-staff and the back-staff 5. John Franklin 6. The Northwest Passage offered an alternate trade route to Asia and the riches of Cathay. 7. the Inuit 8. Martin Frobisher 9. ice 10. the *Gjoa*

Bob Marley

MUSICIAN

Black Americans of Achievement

L E G A C Y E D I T I O N

Muhammad Ali

Maya Angelou

Josephine Baker

Johnnie Cochran

Frederick Douglass

W.E.B. Du Bois

Marcus Garvey

Savion Glover

Alex Haley

Jimi Hendrix

Langston Hughes

Jesse Jackson

Scott Joplin

Coretta Scott King

Martin Luther King, Jr.

Malcolm X

Bob Marley

Thurgood Marshall

Jesse Owens

Rosa Parks

Colin Powell

Chris Rock

Sojourner Truth

Harriet Tubman

Nat Turner

Booker T. Washington

Oprah Winfrey

Black Americans of Achievement

LEGACY EDITION

Bob Marley

MUSICIAN

Sherry Beck Paprocki

CHELSEA HOUSE
PUBLISHERS
An imprint of Infobase Publishing

Chelsea House
An imprint of Infobase Publishing
132 West 31st Street
New York NY 10001

Library of Congress Cataloging-in-Publication Data
Paprocki, Sherry.
Bob Marley / Sherry Paprocki.
p. cm. — (Black Americans of achievement, legacy edition)
Includes bibliographical references (p.) and index.
ISBN 0-7910-9213-5 (hardcover)
1. Marley, Bob. 2. Reggae musicians—Jamaica—Biography. I. Title. II. Series.
ML420.M3313P37 2006
782.421646092—dc22   2006004578

Chelsea House books are available at special discounts when purchased in bulk quantities for businesses, associations, institutions, or sales promotions. Please call our Special Sales Department in New York at (212) 967-8800 or (800) 322-8755.

You can find Chelsea House on the World Wide Web at
http://www.chelseahouse.com

Series and cover design by Keith Trego, Takeshi Takahashi

Printed in the United States of America

Bang Hermitage 10 9 8 7 6 5 4 3 2 1

This book is printed on acid-free paper.

All links and Web addresses were checked and verified to be correct at the time of publication. Because of the dynamic nature of the Web, some addresses and links may have changed since publication and may no longer be valid.

Contents

Celebrating a Musical Legend

Thousands of people crowded into Meskal Square in Addis Ababa, Ethiopia, to celebrate what would have been the sixtieth birthday of the legendary reggae singer Bob Marley. The memory of Marley was powerful, and the music promised to be good. The Africa Unite concert would feature several of Marley's adult children singing their own versions of the music their much-beloved father made popular.

It was a sunny Sunday, February 6, 2005. The festive setting brought thousands of people together. Members of the Marley family flew in from Jamaica and the United States. Fans gathered from far-off places like Israel, Spain, South America, England, and even Japan.

For months, the anticipation of this event had built. Red, gold, and green posters wrapped the lampposts in the city of Addis Ababa. Taxi drivers handed out advertisements for the big event. Even Coca-Cola was a sponsor, flying a banner that

Thousands of fans gathered on February 6, 2005, in Meskal Square (above) in Addis Ababa, Ethiopia, for a concert to commemorate what would have been the sixtieth birthday of reggae musician Bob Marley. The event was billed as the largest concert in Ethiopia.

said "Celebrating African Unity." A giant, inflatable Coke bottle stood nearby.

The Marley family was recognizing its most famous member with a month-long celebration that involved films, a photo exhibition of Marley portraits, ceremonial tree plantings, soccer games, and much more. Some events were charitable, with the goal of raising funds for the victims of a tsunami on December 26, 2004, that had wreaked devastation across the Indian Ocean, from Indonesia to the Somali coastline. Other events involved discussions about the future of Africa, held at a nearby United Nations building. A fancy party was given at a local hotel to raise money for an urban youth center. Bob Marley's wife, Rita, buzzed about the city for weeks in flowing African dresses as she attended the many special events and ceremonies.

On the Sunday of the free Africa Unite concert, people of all ages and backgrounds gathered in the hot sun. Some had been in town for days, participating in the discussions, exhibits, and other events. Others were Ethiopians who came to hear the free music. Some wore T-shirts imprinted with photos of their idol, his trademark long dreadlocks providing an unmistakable image. Others wore jewelry fashioned in the green, gold, and red colors of the Ethiopian flag. Still others wore the flag itself, draped around their shoulders. Ethiopian government officials arrived in limousines, while exiled Ethiopian royalty showed up a bit more quietly. Backstage, Bob Marley's longtime music producer, Chris Blackwell of Island Records, peered out at the crowd in amazement.

THE RASTA PROPHET

Many of the fans who gathered on this day to celebrate Marley's birthday believed that the musician was also a prophet, a symbol of the Rastafarians' Jah, the name that Rastafarians use to refer to their God. The Rastas are devoted followers of a religion rooted in Ethiopia that is based on the tenets of peace, love, and unity. They honored Marley in a way that others honor and praise God in their own religions. There was no physical proof that Marley was or was not the prophet they sought. The large number of Rastafarians who turned out for the celebration, however, caused some concern to local Christian sects.

Local policemen closely watched the throngs of festivalgoers, but the officers' sternness did not dampen the audience's enthusiasm—everyone bounced to the beat when the reggae music began. A few of the expected musical artists did not show up, but no one seemed overly concerned. American singer Lauryn Hill, the partner of one of Marley's sons, Rohan, agreed to break her musical silence and performed three new tunes. Marley's mother, 78-year-old Cedella Booker, went onstage to read a poem she had written as a tribute to her son.

"I never thought I would live to see this day," she later told a newspaper reporter. "I can see that Bob Marley remains the star of the show."

The celebration got off to a riveting start, with Rita Marley leading the crowd in "Happy Birthday, Bob," then joining Marley's former backup singers for a few numbers. After that, five of Marley's sons sang several of his hits, including "Get Up, Stand Up," "I Shot the Sheriff," and "War."

When the celebration was over, Rita Marley called it a huge success: "There has been lots of hard work, lots of energy, lots of faith, lots of tears, lots of happiness. But it has been a dream come true."

Rita Marley, Bob Marley's widow, is shown as she welcomed the Ethiopian prime minister, Meles Zenawi, to the concert in Addis Ababa. "There has been lots of hard work," Rita Marley said about the birthday celebration, "but it's been a dream come true."

THE MUSIC AND THE MESSAGE

In all, it was an extraordinarily festive day that honored the legendary reggae singer. It was a memorial not just to Marley, but also to the slow, rhythmic tunes originated by him and other Jamaican musicians during a time of social change in the 1960s. Marley's reggae music is still loved all over the world for its distinct message.

Marley wrote "Get Up, Stand Up" with fellow musician Peter Tosh as a call-to-arms for the people in poor areas of Jamaica to stand up for their rights. Today, the song's meaning defies political, religious, and personal boundaries. It has sustained its popularity across generational and geographical borders. The organization Amnesty International even follows that theme in its "Get Up, Sign Up" campaign.

Reggae music features the soothing beat of slow rock and blues, mixed in with the familiar calypso sounds that developed their own distinct rhythm. In the beginning, reggae was perhaps more the woeful call of destitute teens who grew up in the slums of Kingston, Jamaica. They played homemade instruments and hoped one day to be able to buy real ones. For these youths, their music was the hope of a better future, one in which they would have a bed to sleep in, plenty of food to eat, and respect—especially respect.

Jamaica was undergoing political upheaval at the time that Marley and other young musicians were mainly concerned with their music. The unfairness with which their people were treated, coupled with the fact that Jamaica was a nation crying for its independence, spilled into their music.

Jamaica has a long history as an island ruled by outsiders. It was claimed by the Spanish in 1494 when Christopher Columbus landed there, but it was taken by the British about 160 years later. During Great Britain's rule, slaves were imported from Africa to work on huge British sugar plantations. When the slaves were emancipated in 1838, many settled into the

Jamaican countryside on small farms. In 1962, Jamaica was granted its independence from Great Britain.

Marley's mother was a rural woman who took her young son to Kingston, Jamaica's capital and largest city, so that she could earn a better living. There, in the Trench Town section of Kingston, Marley's focus was purely on his music even as Jamaica was granted its independence. In the end, it was Marley and others, schooled by a few older Jamaican musicians, who popularized a genre of music, reggae, that celebrates freedom, independence, and unity. As a young man, Marley sang with a group known as the Wailers, and the message of their lives was expressed in several of their hits. Their discontent with excessive police curfews came through their song "Burnin' and Lootin'"; their disgust with police roadblocks with the song "Rebel Music"; and their concern with famine in the slums with their song "Them Belly Full." Though reggae started on this island in the Caribbean Sea, it is now recognized and celebrated around the world.

After years of struggle as a musician, Marley had only begun to enjoy success when he died of cancer at the age of 36. He had refused to accept traditional treatments because they were opposed by his Rastafarian religion. Many of his Rastafarian fans completely understood his choices.

A SYMBOLIC SETTING

Although Jamaica was his birthplace, Marley leaned toward adopting Ethiopia as his spiritual home by the time of his death. The country, in fact, is the base of the Rastafarian religion. Just weeks before his sixtieth birthday celebration, there were reports in the news—later denied by his wife—that Marley's family wished to take his tomb from its resting place in rural Jamaica and place it in Ethiopia.

"It has always been the wish of Bob Marley to return to Ethiopia and become a Rastafarian…," Rita Marley explained to a reporter during the birthday celebration. "And with the African

IN HIS OWN WORDS...

When Bob Marley released his most political album, *Survival*, at a time of increased turmoil in Africa, he had a message for Africans around the world in his song "Africa, Unite." In the United States, his Survival tour opened at the popular Apollo Theater in Harlem in October 1979, causing the community to buzz with excitement after the show. Here is his call in "Africa, Unite":

So Africa, unite 'cause the children wanna come home
Africa, unite 'cause we're moving right out of Babylon
And we're grooving to our father's land

How good and how pleasant it would be
Before God and Man
To see the unification of all Rastaman, yeah

Union, Addis Ababa is the capital of Africa and therefore a very symbolic place," she added. (The African Union, an organization of African nations, is headquartered in Addis Ababa.)

Though his tomb was not moved, the Marley family, for the first time ever, selected this symbolic Ethiopian city to honor the musician during his birthday celebration. Previously, the family held the birthday celebrations in Jamaica. "The message today is that Africa should unite. This is what we're focusing on," his oldest son, Ziggy, explained to a reporter. "We don't listen to the skeptics or hypocrites who speak against the dream of Africans."

Music spilled out over the city that sunny afternoon and into the chilly Ethiopian evening. "Get up, stand up. Stand up for your rights," Ziggy Marley and his brothers sang, as they continued to commemorate the legend of their father.

2

The Garden Parish

Nesta Robert Marley was born on February 6, 1945, in the hamlet of Rhoden Hall, located in the mountainous country of the parish of St. Ann in north-central Jamaica. To residents of the island—which lies south of the eastern end of Cuba—St. Ann is the "garden parish," renowned for its fertile land, natural beauty, and strong-minded, independent inhabitants. For black Jamaicans, it holds special significance as the birthplace of the island's two most prominent heroes, Bob Marley and Marcus Garvey. In the early part of the twentieth century, Garvey earned great fame, as well as political persecution, as an advocate of black self-determination and the "back to Africa" movement. Because of his supposed prediction that blacks should look to Africa for the imminent crowning of a new king who would bring redemption, Garvey is regarded by Rastas as second in importance only to Haile Selassie (1892–1975), the former Ethiopian emperor, who is considered

Marcus Garvey, who was an advocate of black self-determination in the early twentieth century, was born in St. Ann, the "garden parish" of Jamaica. Two of Jamaica's national heroes hailed from St. Ann—Garvey and Bob Marley.

to be the Messiah himself. Garvey's mantle as a prophet would be inherited by Bob Marley.

Marley's mixed ancestry embodied his homeland's tormented colonial past—fitting for someone who would offer his "songs of freedom" as redemption for Jamaica's black sufferers. Under British rule, Jamaica was initially best known as the "pirate capital" of the Caribbean. From its harbors, buccaneers and privateers—pirates granted official license by the English to prey on foreign ships—routinely plundered Spanish vessels. The English had also discovered another source of wealth from the island's natural bounty. Jamaica's climate and topography made it ideal for the production of sugar, for which Europe and the North American colonies seemed to have an inexhaustible appetite. Indeed, demand for the sweetener was so great that it generated profits (in one modern-day historian's estimate) similar to those in the cocaine trade today. Along with the other valuable British possessions in the West Indies, Jamaica became one of a group of islands known as the sugar islands, a huge agricultural factory devoted to the cultivation of sugar cane, the refinement of sugar, and its shipment to North America and Europe as part of the incredibly lucrative "triangle trade."

A TORTURED PAST

In the seventeenth and eighteenth centuries, over one million Africans were forcibly brought across the Atlantic to live, work, and die as slaves in Jamaica's sugar fields. They came from what was known as the Slave Coast, from countries like Ghana, Togo, Benin, and Nigeria. Their labor made the island the largest and richest sugar producer in the Caribbean: From 1673 to 1740, the number of sugar plantations on Jamaica grew from 57 to 430, and the wealth of the white British planter class on the island increased correspondingly.

Dominant economically, politically, and socially, the elite white governing class was never more than a tiny numerical minority in Jamaica. In 1775, for example, Jamaica was inhabited by 13,000 whites and more than 200,000 blacks, virtually all of them slaves. Today, Jamaica's population is estimated at slightly more than 2.7 million people. Less than one percent is white, while 90 percent is black. Just under 10 percent of the population is characterized as mixed in heritage. The whites' small numbers during colonial times, combined with the necessity of maintaining the slave system by the threat and use of brute force and terror, contributed to their siege mentality. Nothing scared them more than the prospect of unified black resistance, whether through armed uprisings or political organization.

The Maroons

In Jamaica, black resistance commonly meant escape to the wilderness—particularly the rugged Blue Mountains in the east and the impenetrable Cockpit Country, the island's west-central region, where the limestone craters resemble the surface of the moon. The people there believed in the establishment of self-governing, self-sufficient communities. The runaway slaves, known to the British as Maroons (from the Spanish word *cimarrón*, which means "wild"), became legendary for their ferocity and craftiness in defending their hard-won freedom. For roughly 50 years, from 1690 to 1739—a time when the red-coated British Army was gaining a reputation as the most formidable fighting force in the world—the Maroons fought the British to a dead standstill.

The Maroons' daring exploits forced the British to grant them freedom on their own land, where by treaty neither the British nor the colonial government would have any legal jurisdiction. The whites, however, used a strategy that would serve them increasingly well in Jamaica over the years: divide and conquer. Aware that a half-century of warfare against a great world power had left the Maroon communities exhausted, the British exploited the disdain that the proud, freedom-loving runaways and their descendants felt for those of their countrymen who "allowed" themselves to remain in slavery. By terms of the peace treaty, the Maroons were obligated to help the British "kill, suppress or destroy" all future black rebels and to track down and return to their masters all runaway slaves. Once an inspiration to black Jamaicans, the Maroons became another feared oppressor.

Black resistance continued. A second, smaller-scale Maroon uprising took place in 1795. The rebellious Maroons succeeded in burning the town of Trelawney to the ground but were soon vanquished, with the surviving rebels shipped into permanent exile in Nova Scotia, Canada.

In 1831, a preacher named Sam Sharpe led the last major slave rebellion on Jamaica. It took the authorities several days to restore order. "Rather death than life as a slave," were the last words uttered by Sharpe as he met his end on the gallows in the town of Montego Bay.

Deliverance for the rest of Sharpe's fellow slaves came three years later, in 1834, when the moral arguments of the island's religious leaders, coupled with the mounting conviction that Jamaica would never know peace as long as the slave system existed, brought about emancipation. Initially, freedom for Jamaica's blacks was only a legal formality, as the newly freed slaves were required to work 40 hours a week for four years for their former masters—for no wages. Finally, in 1838, slavery as a legal institution was officially and genuinely abolished. Relatively few of the former slaves chose to remain on the plantations as contract laborers.

Though the Jamaican sugar industry's peak had passed, the planter class retained economic, political, and social control. Denied the vote and the right to hold political office, blacks had no power to influence the course of the nation. Newly raised from slavery, they lacked the means to obtain land of any significant quantity or quality, the capital to establish businesses, and access to higher education. Control of the island's wealth and opportunity remained where it always had been: with a small white elite, the descendants of Jamaica's colonial rulers.

PARENTS WITH LITTLE IN COMMON

Although he was not a descendant of the 21 families that are thought to have owned most of Jamaica's land, Bob Marley's father was a member of this ruling class. In 1944, Captain Norval Sinclair Marley of the British West Indian Regiment was appointed overseer of British lands in the parish of St. Ann. His duties involved making periodic inspections, on horseback, of the government's huge landholdings in the remote rural area. The job brought him into regular contact with the people of the parish, and he often relied on their hospitality for shelter and food. Captain Marley often stayed in the large house owned by an elderly black woman named Katherine Malcolm (known to her family as Yaya) in the tiny settlement of Nine Mile, so called because of its distance from St. Ann's Bay.

The tale of the middle-aged British officer and the 17-year-old Cedella Malcolm, Yaya's granddaughter, is, according to the son who was born of their relationship, an old and familiar one on the island. "Like you can read it, you know; it's one o' dem slave stories," Bob Marley would say years later, with some bitterness. "White guy get the black woman and breed her." On another occasion, he explained, "I'm born in Babylon. My father, a guy who got together with my mother, he's a English ... a guy who was a captain in the army, go to war. You can't get no more Babylon than that! You know what I mean?" His mother, Marley asserted with considerable pride, was "African, a black woman from way in St. Ann's, way in Jamaica, way in the country."

Bob Marley would say on many occasions that he was "born fatherless." But when Norval Marley learned that Cedella Malcolm was pregnant, he did not immediately abandon her, as men in his position usually did. Instead, to the surprise of nearly everyone, especially his wealthy Kingston family, Norval agreed to marry Cedella and promised to take care of her and their son. The wedding took place on June 9, 1944, but by then Norval was having second thoughts. Immediately before the wedding, he told his bride that he was going away soon—the next day in fact—to Kingston, where he was taking a new job as a foreman on a construction project. Cedella was not to come with him or join him later; his family would not like it. He promised, however, to visit her every weekend and support his son.

Predictably, Norval made few visits during Cedella's pregnancy, and he appeared even less often once his mother and his brother learned of the marriage and threatened to disinherit him. After the birth of the boy, Cedella saw her husband on only a handful of occasions. Norval bestowed the name of Nesta Robert on the seven-pound, four-ounce infant—Robert after his brother and Nesta for reasons unexplained. He continued to send money for a brief time, but he visited for only one purpose—to convince Cedella that she should surrender her boy to him to be raised in Kingston.

"Never you ever let him take that child from you," Cedella's father, Omeriah Malcolm, warned. Though poor by the standards of white Jamaicans, living in a crude cabin of plaster and zinc, Omeriah Malcolm was the most prosperous and respected farmer in the Nine Mile region. On his lands high in the mountains, he grew coffee, bananas, mangoes, pimentos, oranges, yams, and tangerines, which he hauled to market in a donkey-drawn cart or an old truck. He also owned a small grocery store, a bakery, and a dry-goods store. Descended from the Cromanty people of Ghana, the Malcolms, like several other families in the area, had resided in the vicinity of Nine Mile since the early seventeenth century, living and working as tenant slaves until emancipation, then helping to establish the free village of blacks that even today appears on few maps; it is far from the area's only paved road, which connects the village of Alexandria and the town of Claremont.

THE MYALMAN

Much more than his farming success and his ancestry made Omeriah Malcolm the most respected citizen of Nine Mile. He was also revered as a *myalman*, a kind of benevolent conjurer or healer trained in the Jamaican folk religion, *kumina*. Just as the patois spoken by Jamaican blacks was English overlaid with numerous African grammatical formulations, usages, and words, so too the religious faith of rural Jamaican blacks was a blend of Christianity and traditional customs, practices, and beliefs deeply rooted in the African heritage of the people.

The most important rituals were those associated with *obeah*, which comes from an African word meaning "magic" or "sorcery." The obeahman used his learning in the magical arts to harness and exploit the powers of the *duppies*, the mischievous, potentially malignant spirits of the dead. The obeahman was a figure of power in the community, someone to be respected, even feared. In the time of the slaves, the obeahman was the protector of the oppressed, their avenger against the whites; now, more often, he was seen as a malignant influence.

The myalman was a more positive practitioner of the mystic arts. Where the obeahman might enlist duppies to inflict harm or even kill someone, the myalman used his learning to counteract such negative influences. The myalman believed that the power of the spirit world should be used only to do good; he knew the curative and magical powers of the infinite variety of herbs and plants that grew in the Jamaican bush, and he could mix them into potions, fashion amulets, and perform rituals that could protect a person from duppies or even old Screwface himself, as rural Jamaicans sometimes called Satan.

When Cedella became pregnant, Omeriah Malcolm cautioned her to heed the Jamaican belief that expectant mothers were particularly vulnerable to the work of malignant spirits. "Always remember," he would say, "you are between life and death until you give birth to that baby." He also taught Cedella which herbs could ease the discomforts of pregnancy and childbirth and which plant leaves were suitable for cleaning the new baby's delicate skin. When four-month-old Nesta suddenly took ill, it was Omeriah who concluded that the baby's vomiting and seizures were the work of Screwface. "Somebody science him," he said, "put duppy on the boy." After consulting with Yaya, his equally knowledgeable mother, Omeriah prepared a potion of nearly a dozen herbs. When fed to Nesta, the potion quickly caused the illness to lift.

Fans of Bob Marley's discuss the influence of his music at the entrance to Marley's grave at Nine Mile in St. Ann. Bob Marley lived the first six years of his life in rural Nine Mile, before his father persuaded his mother to send him to the Jamaican capital of Kingston. After a year, he was back in Nine Mile.

According to reports of his childhood, it wasn't long before people were noticing that the small, dark-eyed boy had unusual powers of his own. Several qualities set him apart, aside from his light skin tone and white ancestry (neither of which was seen with particular favor by the people of Nine Mile, who were extremely proud of their African heritage). There was his quietness, for example; for a boy of four or five, Nesta seemed unusually thoughtful, with a penetrating stare that seemed to be searching for whatever secrets lay hidden beneath the surface of things. Combined with his obvious intelligence, his gaze made adults, even his mother, somewhat uneasy. He seemed to prefer to spend much of his time alone, lost in thought; many were the times that Cedella, walking along some dusty path through the bush to or from the fields, would be startled to come upon spindly, barefoot Nesta, sitting contemplatively under a tree or on a rock. "What are you doing," she would ask him, "do you not fear the blackheart man?" (The blackheart man is an evil spirit, not unlike a bogeyman, who is said by Jamaicans to prey upon disobedient or careless little children.) And always, she said, her son would respond only with "a smile so blue-swee," meaning cunning, knowing, or elusive.

A YOUNG BOY'S POWERS

Then there was the fortune-telling. Cedella was not especially surprised when neighbors began to tell her that they regularly went to Nesta, a child of five, to have their palms read. The boy, they insisted, told them things about themselves that he could not possibly have known, and he made predictions that invariably came true. "The finger of the Lord is upon the boy," his grandfather proclaimed. "Him a manchild with powers that may grow or may fade." It was an opinion that his mother soon came to share, a harbinger of what was to come. Years later, she recalled:

How he do things and prophesy things, he is not just by himself—he have higher powers, even from when he is a little boy. The way I felt, the kind of vibes I get when Bob comes around.... It's too honorable. I always look upon him with great respect: there is something inside telling me that he is not only a son—there is something greater in this man. Bob is of a small stature, but when I hear him talk, he talk big. When it comes to the feelings and reactions I get from Bob, it was always too spiritual to even mention or talk about. Even from when he was a small child coming up.

In few ways did the boy seem typical. He was independent, yet rarely disobedient; he knew his own mind but seldom argued; he was solitary but made friends easily; he was confident, yet shy. He started school at age four, a year earlier than normal, because the teacher said he had the intelligence of a child twice his age. Later he would say, "Me not have education, me have inspiration. If I was educated I would be a damn fool." Yet his teachers remember a student of rare ability, who blossomed when he was given attention: The penetrating stare disguised a gentle nature that craved love and affection and was perhaps more easily hurt than he let on. "As he was shy," one of his teachers, Clarice Bushey, recalled, "if he wasn't certain he was right, he wouldn't always try. In fact, he hated to get answers wrong, so sometimes you'd really have to draw the answer out of him. And then give him a clap, he liked that, the attention." To Bushey, it was clear that Nesta received a lot of love and kindness at home: "I imagined he must have been very much a mother's pet, because he would only do well if you gave him large amounts of attention. But it was obvious he had a lot of potential. When he came by you to your desk, you knew he just wanted to be touched and held; he was really quite soft. It seemed like a natural thing with him—what he was used to."

In other ways he seemed an ordinary Jamaican child of his time and place. When not in school, he spent his time, as did the other children of Nine Mile, in the fields with his mother and the rest of the large, extended Malcolm family, fetching water and performing other chores. Very early in the morning and in the evenings, he might be expected to round up and feed the chickens and goats; at any hour he could be seen riding along the steep mountain paths to the fields on his pet donkey, Nimble. Most characteristically, he could be found improvising a game of football. Nesta was crazy about football—known as soccer in the United States—and would play anywhere, anytime, with anyone; if a ball was not available, an orange might do, or a tin can, or a gourd. If playmates were not around, he would play by himself.

There was only one thing Nesta loved more than football: music. It has been said that in Jamaica one can literally breathe in melodies with the sweet tropical air, and little Nesta was truly surrounded by music. One of Omeriah's brothers played violin, guitar, and banjo with several of the semiprofessional groups that made dance music at various parish gatherings. Omeriah himself played violin and accordion; even more important, he owned a "sound system"—a turntable, oversize speakers, and an amplifier. Cedella, too, was a musician, a gifted vocalist who sang in the Shiloh Apostolic Church choir and even gave several gospel concerts around St. Ann.

Cedella sang to Nesta constantly, and the boy heard music at home and in the fields, where it made the work go easier, as well as in church and at communal social gatherings. He heard hymns and spirituals; work songs, with their rhythmic calls and responses; popular tunes on his grandfather's sound system; old mournful folk songs, the kind Cedella's mother used to sing; and the raucous reels and stomps of the homebred Jamaican music known as quadrille, played by the string bands with which his uncle performed. Of all the children in his school, he was the most creative maker of musical instruments, crafting a guitar out of a sardine box, a piece of wood, and some baling wire, and then somehow coaxing melodic sounds from it. His soft, somewhat high-pitched singing voice made even more of an impression. "During school break," he told an American reporter in 1977, "the teacher, she say, 'Who can talk, talk; who can make anything, make; who can sing, sing'; and me sing." But his musical calling had begun far earlier than that, he explained—had begun, in fact, the moment he entered the world. "How did you start out in singing?" he was asked. "Started out ... crying," he replied. "Yeah, started out crying, you know?"

LIFE IN KINGSTON

When Nesta was about six years old, his father persuaded his mother to send him to Kingston, promising the bright young

Bob Marley would come a long way from his childhood in Nine Mile to this concert in 1979. As a boy, he created makeshift instruments, like a guitar made from a sardine box, a piece of wood, and baling wire.

boy access to the city's finer educational system. Reluctantly, after consulting with her father, Cedella agreed, with the understanding that she was not relinquishing custody and could visit her son whenever she liked. In Kingston, Nesta received more of an education outside the classroom, absorbing lessons about the bleak social conditions plaguing Jamaica's poor, which would deeply influence his music and his worldview.

In the 1950s, tens of thousands of black Jamaicans came to Kingston—primarily to the shantytowns that were springing up in the western part of the city—in search of economic opportunities not available to them in the country. With the majority of Jamaica's land held by a tiny white economic elite, most blacks in the countryside lived on and worked relatively small plots of property. Over time, the size of those plots was further diminished by inheritance, and the quality of the soil suffered from hard use. Added to these difficulties were the eternal crises that small farmers face—low prices, foreign competition, rising costs of supplies and provisions, and unfavorable weather. Year by year, there was less good land for Jamaica's rural population. Overall, an estimated half of the Jamaican population earned less than $10 a week. For these reasons, an increasingly educated and mobile rural population found itself eager to explore the experiences and opportunities that Kingston had to offer.

But very few found Kingston to be the promised land. More often, it was called the "house of bondage" by the suffering inhabitants of Trench Town. The sites and names of the various West Kingston shantytowns give some indication of the quality of life there. Trench Town sprang up over and around the municipal sewer ditch (or trench) that drained the waste of the older part of the city. Another community, Dungle, named as a Jamaican contraction for Dung Hill, was built atop a municipal garbage dump. Back O' the Wall spread out behind the wall of the public cemetery.

For obvious reasons, the residents of these areas referred to themselves as "sufferers" or, sometimes, "Israelites" (like the Jews in the Old Testament book of Exodus, they were waiting to be led out of exile in the wilderness). There was no electricity or running water in Trench Town, and the cooling breezes from the mountains never blew down there, reportedly leaving it the hottest spot in Jamaica. The residents lived in hovels, shelters, and shanties cobbled together from a fantastic assortment of materials: discarded wood, packing crates, corrugated tin, gasoline cans, newspapers, driftwood gathered from the beaches of Kingston Bay, barrels, oil drums, fruit crates, and whatever else could be scavenged from the Dungle. Jobs were even harder to come by than they were in the countryside; harder still to maintain, in the eyes of some, was the dignified self-sufficiency of the rural Jamaican. The shacks of Trench Town crowded together one after another; the people cooked outside over open fires in communal yards; they washed outside with water from standpipes or from the sewage ditches, where they also relieved themselves. Pigs, goats, and chickens roamed free.

The more fortunate residents of Trench Town lived in "government yards"—public housing built by the British government after the great hurricane of 1951 blew most of the shanties away. The government yards were simple concrete or stucco buildings, a couple of stories tall, usually built in a horseshoe shape around a sometimes-gated communal yard. Each building might contain a dozen or so apartments, each with a couple of rooms. In the more luxurious places, two apartments generally shared a kitchen, and several apartments would share whatever indoor bathroom facilities there were. More often, cooking was done outside in the yard, where residents also washed up at a communal standpipe. Marley would memorialize the essentially communal life lived in these government yards in perhaps his most famous song, "No Woman, No Cry."

Norval Marley, as a member of the white ruling class, lived in the better part of Kingston, but that did not make his son's life any easier. As soon as Nesta arrived in the city, his father surrendered him to the custody of a family friend, an old, sickly white woman whom the boy knew only as Mrs. Grey. Nesta stayed with her for about a year, fetching her groceries and coal and running other errands, sporadically attending school, and all the time wondering why his mother did not come to look for him. Cedella, meanwhile, was frantic with worry; after initially giving her placid assurances about Nesta's well-being, Norval Marley steadfastly refused to tell her of the boy's whereabouts. Eventually, though, Cedella and her son were reunited, and Nesta returned to St. Ann and to his old life.

"He was very handy to Mrs. Grey," Cedella later told Stephen Davis, a Marley biographer, "and the two of them helped each other. You could see she was helping him from her heart. But he told us right away he wanted to go home."

Back in St. Ann, Nesta resumed the old routine of school, chores, and football. Those closest to him noticed a change, however; he seemed even more serious than before. He quickly lost the weight he had gained in the city and in fact became dangerously thin, as if something was burning away from within him. When asked, he now refused to read palms, telling those who had asked that he had found a new way to prophesy: His talents were all to be devoted to music. "No," he would say, "I'm not reading no more hand: I'm singing now." With her father's help, Cedella had opened up a little grocery store, and customers there would often pay Nesta to sing for them.

Despite his return to the countryside, Nesta's life was some-what unsettled. Still very young, Cedella was trying to find herself and became increasingly dissatisfied with the quiet life of St. Ann. As she tried various situations in different towns, her son was often entrusted to the care of relatives. Though they were certainly more trustworthy than his father, who died in 1955, Nesta nonetheless missed the company and care of his mother.

Finally, in 1957, Cedella decided to move to Kingston. "Oh, I just had to get out of the country," she told Stephen Davis. "Every young girl in St. Ann want to come out of the country and, you know, shake up themself a little bit. So I want to go to Kingston and try also." Initially, she stayed with various relatives in West Kingston and tried to find stable work. In a short time, she set up house in a one-room apartment with Thaddeus "Taddy" Livingston, a married man (who was not living with his wife) she had become romantically involved with back in St. Ann.

3

Surviving in Trench Town

Cedella Marley and Taddy Livingston were able to get government housing at 19 Second Street in Trench Town in 1957. They were soon joined by her son, who by then preferred the name Bob to his childhood name of Nesta. Finding the money to pay Bob's private school tuition always presented a challenge, but one that Cedella willingly met each term. "I never have to beg nobody or borrow from nobody," she proudly recalled.

> I could pay his fee, then save again to buy his shoes. I can't remember a time when I was so badly off that I couldn't find food for him. And he was not a child that demand this or demand that. Never have no problem with him: always obedient, would listen to me. Sometimes he get a little mad with me, but it never last for time.

Also joining the makeshift family in Trench Town was Neville "Bunny" Livingston, Taddy Livingston's oldest son, who was two years younger than Bob. The two had become close friends in St. Ann and were stepbrothers of a sort: Although Cedella Marley and Taddy Livingston never married, they had a daughter, Pearl, in 1962. Together, the family faced the difficult life of Trench Town.

"RUDE BOYS" REBELLION

Always independent, Bob now found excitement in the city streets that kept him away from home. It was a lot easier here to round up a group of boys for a football game, for example, and Bob still loved the sport. In Trench Town, though, more illicit activities abounded. Hanging out with the guys could easily progress into trouble with the law. With their future prospects seemingly so dim, West Kingston youth were quick to act out their frustration. By the early 1960s, the "rude boys" of the West Kingston ghetto had become Jamaica's most troubling social phenomenon. Inspired by American gangster films, martial arts flicks, and the spaghetti Westerns of directors like Sergio Leone, they celebrated criminal behavior, pointless violence, and disrespect toward all established authority as the only means of rebellion available to them. The "rudie's" weapon of choice was the ratchet knife, a curved German-made switchblade, and if the liquor-store holdup or his latest marijuana deal netted him enough cash, he preferred to dress in gangster finery—broad-brimmed hats, thin ties, and platform shoes.

Although he was never a rude boy himself, Bob came from the same tough environment, and he certainly had rudies among his friends. It was next to impossible not to, if someone wanted to get by; it was the rare West Kingston family that never had a member in trouble with the law. Trench Town mothers considered that they had defied the odds if their boys made it to 14—the age in Jamaica at which lower-class youths usually quit school—without landing in jail.

Although no stranger to the roughest aspects of Trench Town life, Bob had qualities that seemed to guide him through

Cedella Marley Booker, Bob Marley's mother, sent a kiss to the audience after performing in February 2005 at city hall in Addis Ababa, Ethiopia. When Bob was 12, he and his mother moved to the Trench Town section of Kingston. About her son, Cedella said, "He was not a child that demand this or demand that. Never have no problem with him: always obedient, would listen to me."

safely. Despite being quite small and generally soft-spoken, he still exuded an aura that deterred people from messing with him. His slightness was combined with a wiry strength, and his skill in football won him much respect. His thoughtfulness made his few words—when he spoke—much more powerful. And, he exhibited intelligence and charisma that made others pay attention to what he said. Usually gentle, he could be fierce if the situation required it. When pushed, he pushed back, and he never backed down. On the street they called him the Tuff Gong, and it was said that if you wanted to start something with him, you had better be prepared to finish it, because he would be sure to do so.

Cedella tried to steer Bob away from the streets, but with little success. Occupied with her own struggle, she did not have as much time to spend with him as she would have liked, and as he grew older, her strong-minded boy became even harder to control. "Bob, these people, these boys who are around you, seem like bad boys," she once warned. "A man is known by the company he keeps."

"Yes, Mama, they *are* bad boys," Bob replied. "But I not going do nothing that is wrong, you know?"

"I know you ain't going do nothing that is wrong," Cedella said, "but *these people* can go do bad and because you're in their company, they might lead the police to believe you are in league with them."

"Mama, they don't tell me what to do," Bob insisted. "Nobody can get me into any trouble. My friends, I tell *them* what to do."

As his songs would demonstrate, Bob fully grasped the despair, the hopelessness, the poverty, and the waste of ghetto life, but he experienced—and expressed—the many other more positive aspects of everyday existence there that the upper class of Jamaica always overlooked: joy, wisdom, kindness, generosity, dignity, and beauty. "Me grow stubborn you know," Marley later explained of his coming of age in Trench Town. "Me grow without mother or father. Me no have no parent for have no big influence upon me. Me just grow in the ghetto with the youth. Stubborn, no obey no one; but we had qualities, and we were good to one another."

THE MUSIC IN THE AIR

Trench Town was undeniably rich in music. For the sufferers, music was perhaps the most affordable form of entertainment, as well as the most accessible means of expression. Bob Marley had sustained his love for music—he made his singing debut in 1959 at a Queens Theatre talent show, where he won a pound (roughly the equivalent of five dollars) and listened to a wide variety of styles. By the late 1950s, even some of the poorest Jamaicans could afford a cheap transistor radio, and at night in the yards, with the wind blowing from the north, American radio stations—from Miami and even New Orleans—came in clear. Arriving over the airwaves was American rhythm and blues, as performed by artists like Brook Benton, Ray Charles, Fats Domino, and Ruth Brown. Especially popular with young Jamaicans were the harmonies of male vocal groups like the Moonglows, the Impressions, and Marley's beloved Drifters. The silky vocals of Nat King Cole and Sam Cooke were favorites, as were the somewhat more exuberant jump blues of Louis Jordan; the flamboyant, pioneering rock and roll of Little Richard; and the relentless funk of James Brown. Even American country music was admired, with Jim Reeves, the East Texas hillbilly with the celebrated "touch of velvet" in his voice, somewhat improbably claiming a wide following among black Jamaicans. The hundreds of thousands of Jamaicans who immigrated to the United States to find work were assured the warmest welcome when they returned home if they brought with them a batch of the latest records from the American charts.

Proprietors who trucked in huge sound systems supplied the residents of West Kingston with up-to-the-minute music. On weekends, these sound-system owners would stage "jump-ups," as the huge outdoor dances were called. Hundreds, even thousands, of the sufferers would come together to dance to the booming sounds, socialize with one another, and eat and drink. The sound-system proprietors and their disc jockeys were the first stars of the fledgling Jamaican music industry. The DJs did much more than cue up records on turntables. They had to work the crowd, understanding its mood and gauging a sequence of songs that would keep everyone in the groove, letting people simmer down as their energy began to flag, and then raising the temperature to a boil with a new track. Using several turntables, the DJ might segue from a popular instrumental section of one hit right into the rhythm groove of another, creating, in a sense, a new track. In between songs, over a repeating instrumental riff maintained by holding the turntable arm in a desired place so it did not progress across the vinyl, or over a so-called dub track (an instrumental version of a popular song), the DJ would improvise rhymes, often boastful proclamations of his sexual prowess, ribald tales, commentary on events in the community, exhortations to the dancers, or putdowns of rival sound-system operators. The sound-system dances were one of the birthplaces of today's rap music.

By the late 1950s, the sound-system proprietors began to set up their own recording studios to capitalize on the rich local talent. There was a wealth of exceptional musicians who had little opportunity to record, so the operators were able to establish a stranglehold on the Jamaican recording industry, paying new artists cut-rate flat fees for a record without royalties. In other words, musicians were barely making any money from their deals with these promoters. Among the newest generation of aspiring Jamaican musicians—the youths who were inspired by the new sounds from America and had created the fast-paced hybrid known as ska—the desire to make records, even on such one-sided terms, was fierce.

No one was more driven in this regard than Bob Marley. The many influences he had been exposed to in the city—musical and otherwise—had only intensified his love of music, sparked his creativity and imagination, and inflamed his ambition. When he left school at 14, his mother found him a position as an apprentice welder, despite his desire to devote all his energies to music. After a short time on the job, a tiny steel splinter became embedded in his eye, and the injury settled the issue for good. Cedella later told the writer Malika Lee Whitney, "[At the hospital] him say, 'You no hear me say is nothing else me want to do beside sing?' And I have to say, 'Really, is true.'"

REGGAE COLLEGE

So Bob Marley became a full-time student in the "reggae college," as some would later call the streets of Trench Town. If reggae did not yet exist as a distinct musical form, the seeds of its
development were being planted in West Kingston. Among
those doing the planting was a singer, regarded as perhaps
Jamaica's finest, named Joe Higgs, who lived in a yard right
behind the Marleys. Higgs had recorded several hits, but
because of the erratic payment practices of the Jamaican recording industry, even the top musicians seldom earned enough to
move out of the yards. (Higgs, for example, received a flat fee of
$20 for each record he made.) In any event, Higgs was a remark-
ably able teacher, a man genuinely dedicated to imparting his
love and knowledge of music to those serious about learning.
For no other compensation than the joy of teaching and making music, Higgs held nightly gatherings of Jamaican singers
and musicians and coached those just starting out.

Marley was among the most talented and serious beginners,
along with his constant companion, Bunny Livingston. The two,
who still made music with makeshift guitars fashioned out of a
bamboo staff, strands of electrical wire, and a large sardine can,
were regular participants in Higgs's sessions, which often lasted
all night. Higgs taught these youths the principles of harmony,
rhythm, and melody, as well as how to learn from music seemingly far removed from their own. A demanding teacher, Higgs
counseled Marley to listen to modern jazz artists like John
Coltrane. At first, Marley could not understand jazz, but at
Higgs's insistence, he kept on listening. "Me try to get into the
mood where the moon is blue and see the feeling expressed,"
Marley said, using the creative syntax of the Jamaican patois. "Joe
Higgs helped me understand that music. He taught me many
things. Him, y'know, is one heavy music man, Joe Higgs."

Under Higgs's tutelage, Marley's musical development was
rapid. As much as he had talent, he had seriousness and ambition
in his favor; more than the other youths around, he seemed to

know exactly what he wanted to do. Reminiscences of the period, starting with his own, provide a consistent characterization: a single-minded boy sure of his destination, if not always of the exact way to reach it. "Then we used to sing in the back of Trench Town," Marley recalled, "and rehearse plenty until the Drifters came upon the scene, and me love group singing so me just say, well, me have for go look a group."

BIRTH OF THE WAILERS

The first member of that group, of course, was Livingston. The two "spars" (close friends) found a third soulmate during the sessions at Higgs's yard. Tall, extroverted, and angry, carrying himself like a rudie, Hubert Winston McIntosh had a genuine acoustic guitar and called himself Peter Tosh. Under Higgs's direction, the three began honing their skills. Although the group in these early days would sometimes feature other members—like Junior Braithwaite and Beverly Kelso—and perform under different names, the Wailers had been born. "The word *wail* means 'to cry' or 'to moan,'" Tosh later explained. "We were living in this so-called ghetto. No one to help the people. We felt we were the only ones who could express their feelings through music, and because of that the people loved it. So we did it."

Long before the Wailers ever played a gig or made a record, Marley was treating their music as a profession. Livingston and Tosh were extremely strong-willed, but Marley was even more focused. As Higgs recalled,

> Bob was the leader of the group.... Bob needed to know about everything, but he was quick. It was kind of difficult to get the group to be precise in their sound and put it over in their harmony structure. Just took a couple of years to get that perfect. But person to person, they were each capable of leading at any time because I wanted each person to be a leader in his own right, able to lead anyone, or to be able to wail. That is where the concept came from.

As Higgs indicated, the Wailers formed a special vocal mixture. Each of the three main members was able to handle the lead vocals on a particular song, and in harmony their voices blended together with a naturalness that belied their countless hours of training and rehearsal. Tosh's voice was a deep, rumbling baritone, Livingston's a virtual falsetto; together the two were likened to Jerry Butler and Curtis Mayfield of the Impressions. Marley, meanwhile, sang between the two, in a somewhat willowy tenor that was remarkably expressive.

He also had the greatest ability as a songwriter. When he wasn't rehearsing, he would spend his time alone with his guitar, devising melodies and lyrics. In crowded Trench Town, genuine solitude, of the kind conducive to artistic creativity, was often difficult to come by. As she recalled for Marley's biographers Adrian Boot and Chris Salewicz, Pauline Morrison was among a group of students at this time who met Marley each day as they returned home from school. Every afternoon they would encounter him as he sat under the shade of a huge tree, working out his songs on his primitive guitar. Although she remembers him as polite and easygoing, she noticed a reserve, a part of himself that he only expressed through music. "It was always the man and his guitar," she said. "It was very rare you could just sit with him and be with him. Because he was a very moody person, the way I see him. Him is very moody. If people were sitting together with him, he would suddenly just get up and go somewhere else. Just to be by himself."

No doubt some of the moodiness Morrison observed was loneliness. Around the time he was forming the Wailers, Marley fell in love for the first time, with a girl who was a neighbor in his yard. Their romance was short-lived, however, because the girl's older brother objected to Marley's mixed ancestry and insisted that she end the relationship. As Cedella recalled, "Her brother say to Bob, 'We don't want no white man in our breed.'... Her family kill off the romance. Them style Bob as a white man."

According to his mother, it was not the only time Marley was made to suffer because of his ancestry. He "bore a sacrifice" because of his white paternity, she said, and the frequent insults he endured contributed to the air of sorrow that some saw in him. "Sometimes he'd come across the resistance of being half-caste," she recalled:

> There was a problem with his counterparts: having come through this white father caused such difficulties that he'd want to kill himself and think, "Why am I this person? Why is my father white and not black like everybody else? What did I do wrong?" He was lost in that: not being able to have anyone to say it's not your fault, or that there's nothing wrong in being like you are. But that was the atmosphere he came up in, that Trench Town environment where everybody is rough.

Marley suffered an even greater loss soon after. With the birth of her daughter, Pearl, in 1962, Cedella at last determined that there was little future in her relationship with Thaddeus Livingston. She decided, as so many Jamaicans would during the 1960s, to immigrate to the United States. She planned to make her new home in the small city of Wilmington, Delaware, where some of her relatives lived among the Jamaican immigrant community there. She wanted Bob to come with her and even obtained the documents he would need.

But Marley wanted to stay in Jamaica. He had his music now, and that was the most important thing to him; he was 18 and ready to stand on his own. Promising to join his mother at some unspecified time in the near future, Marley bid her farewell.

ON HIS OWN IN TRENCH TOWN

He was homeless, without a job or any source of steady income, but Trench Town youths were used to looking out for one another. One of Marley's closest friends was a young man named

Vincent Ford, whom everyone called Tartar. Four years older than Marley, Tartar had gone out on his own at an earlier age. As a teenager, Tartar had earned his living as a chef at a boys' school, but by this time he made money from the little "kitchen" he set up in his yard on First Street. One of many such unlicensed, unofficial establishments in Trench Town, Ford's kitchen, called the "casbah" by his friends, sold the Jamaican equivalent of fast food—calaloo, dumplings, roast yam, and breadfruit. Much later in the evenings, the kitchen table would be cleared for some gambling, which typically would go on almost until morning. Then the table would be cleared again, and Marley would finally have a place to sleep.

In the hours after midnight, Marley would sit near the huge bonfire that was always kept burning in Tartar's yard, playing

Bob Marley lived in this home in Trench Town, where he began singing with the Wailers. As his songs made clear, Marley captured the despair and poverty of ghetto life, but he also expressed the positive side of everyday existence, the joy and dignity that others often overlooked.

guitar and singing by the dancing firelight. Livingston was usually there with him, and Tosh, and sometimes Braithwaite. A somewhat older man, George Headley Robinson, whom everyone called Georgie, took responsibility for maintaining the fire and taking care of the musicians. A fisherman, he built the fire each night and stoked it with driftwood he picked up while working. The day's catch was offered to feed the musicians and those who gathered to listen, and Georgie "would sit there shirtless all night," Tartar said, "tending the flames as they played." When they woke in the morning, Georgie would brew a huge kettle of bush tea and a communal bowl of cinnamon-flavored cornmeal porridge.

No words could capture the sorrowful joy of those times better than Marley's most beloved song, "No Woman, No Cry," a musical evocation of that period in his life when the sadness of the have-nots was tempered by hope; when loneliness was alleviated by true friendship uncomplicated by material concerns; when a mood of despair could be lifted by a simple song; when the struggle was redeemed by a sharing of the burden. Marley knew, amid the crime, poverty, and desolation, that there were also values all too often overlooked, truths lost in the pursuit of progress. "Good friends we have had, oh good friends we've lost along the way / In this bright future you can't forget your past / So dry your tears, I say … And everything's gonna be alright," he would write in "No Woman, No Cry," remaining firmly in touch with the sufferers at a time when his stardom was on the rise. Georgie was mentioned by name in the lyrics, and Marley gave his composer's credit for the song to Tartar, who had by then become disabled by diabetes. The song held a special place not only in the hearts of Marley's fans but in his own heart. "Me really love 'No Woman, No Cry,'" Marley later said, "because it mean so much to me, so much feeling me get from it. Really love it."

4

Too Hot

The joy of making music in Trench Town, though, was dampened by the huge frustration of doing business in the Jamaican music industry. Marley experienced this aggravation before the Wailers even made their first recordings. In 1961, when he was 16 and just starting to organize the Wailers, Marley met Leslie Kong, a Chinese-Jamaican restaurateur who also owned his own record label, which was called Beverley's. In just a couple of years, Kong had released many Jamaican songs.

Apparently, Marley hung around Beverley's record store, pestering the staff for a chance to sing for the boss, but he was always rebuffed. At that point, either musicians Jimmy Cliff or Derrick Morgan convinced Kong that he ought to listen to Marley sing. Marley recorded a half-dozen or so of his songs at Kong's Federal Studio. "Judge Not" was the first to be released, under the name Robert Marley. Marley was still many years from embracing Rastafari, but the song nonetheless anticipated the moral concerns and biblical tone of his greatest work. "While you talk about me," the song warns, "someone else is judging you." It was followed by "Terror" backed with "One Cup of Coffee," which were released under the name of Bobby Martell. Kong had taken it upon himself—without consulting Marley—to change his name.

None of the songs did particularly well, and Marley was paid the paltry sum of $20 for his musical work. He had difficulty collecting even that and quickly broke off the relationship with Kong, feeling exploited. "We will work together again someday," the willful singer predicted to the producer, "and you will make a lot of money off of me, but you will never be able to enjoy it." Kong had a reputation as a tough character who did not scare easily, but Marley's words unnerved him. Kong felt he had been told something that Marley somehow mysteriously knew with a deep inner certainty. The story would make the rounds in Trench Town for a long time.

The discouraging experience with Kong only spurred Marley's determination to make the Wailers a success. Marley played a handful of solo shows. Some observers, like Derrick Morgan, thought that he was a better dancer than a singer, but he devoted most of his energies to his endless rehearsal sessions with Joe Higgs and the Wailers. For nearly two years, the group's only reward for its hard work was the certainty that it was getting better. But for Marley, the hard times were getting even harder. Tartar's boundless hospitality often left his kitchen too crowded for Marley to stay there, and the singer spent a six-month period living on the streets, sneaking onto rooftops at night to sleep, sometimes staying for a day or two at one of the small Rasta colonies on the beaches.

AN AUDITION

Finally, in late December 1963, Alvin Patterson brought the Wailers to audition for Clement "Sir Coxsone" Dodd at

Dodd's Studio One in the northernmost part of Trench Town. Patterson, whom the Wailers called "Seeco," was recognized as one of the island's master musicians. A constant participant in the sessions at Higgs's yard and a great booster of the Wailers, Patterson was a virtuoso in the traditional Jamaican folk music of *burru* drumming, which uses three drums. Derived from African tradition, burru drumming had been done in the Jamaican countryside to welcome home liberated prisoners, and modern practitioners like Patterson sought ways to incorporate elements of burru into Jamaican popular music.

Dodd, meanwhile, was perhaps the single most important figure in the Jamaican music industry. A pioneering sound-system operator, one of the first to make great use of American records, Dodd was also one of the first to branch out into music production on his own. Known for his idiosyncrasies— he addressed all men as "Jackson," for example—Dodd was as talented as he was eccentric. Though not a musician himself, Dodd was blessed, said the great Jamaican guitarist Ernest Ranglin, with "an extraordinary pair of ears," and an ability to communicate musical ideas in language that musicians could translate into new sounds. "He was really the man," Ranglin said, "the man who came up with the ideas. But he couldn't play, so he would come and explain it to us. After explaining it, I always knew what the man wanted."

The "us" Ranglin referred to was the superb house band Dodd assembled at Studio One, consisting of, among others, Ranglin and Jah Jerry on guitars; trombonist Don Drummond (whom the masterful American jazz pianist George Shearing classified as one of the top jazz musicians in the world); saxophonists Roland Alphonso, Tommy McCook, and Lester Sterling; Johnny "Dizzy" Moore on trumpet; Lloyd Knibbs on drums; Lloyd Brevett and Cluett Johnson on bass; and Jackie Mittoo on keyboards. Eventually these musicians would form a group called the Skatalites. Having tired of the American sounds that many Jamaican artists persisted in imitating, Dodd was looking for something more homegrown.

"I need something to get away from these blues," Dodd put it to Ranglin one day. What Ranglin and his colleagues were developing was ska, an extremely fast-paced rhythmic sound, accentuated with jazzlike horns, that emphasized the off beat. Ska combined the best features of contemporary Jamaican and American music, particularly in its intensity and intricate vocal harmonies. Various explanations are offered for the derivation of the name. Ranglin said ska was essentially a nonsense word coined by musicians "to talk about the *skat! skat! skat!* scratchin' guitar strum that goes behind the rest of the music." Others say the name came from "skavoovee," a slang term of approval then popular in Jamaica and often used by bassist Cluett "Clue-J" Johnson, who helped Ranglin create the sound. Similarly, the peculiar, entrancing qualities of the music were said to be the result of the musicians' attempt to emulate the way the nighttime music from the United States faded in and out on the cheap transistor radios in the West Kingston yards. Ranglin provided another source of origin as well: "We just wanted it to sound like the theme music from one of those westerns that were on TV all the time in the late 1950s."

Ska was the sound that dominated Marley's first recordings for Leslie Kong and most of the records the Wailers would make for Clement Dodd at Studio One. The group auditioned for Dodd beneath the mango tree in the dusty yard behind the studio. Impressed by their vocal sophistication and evident seriousness, Dodd was even more taken by the original material they sang for him, especially "Simmer Down," a song that addressed the escalating violence of the rude boys. Still searching, as always, for authentic Jamaican music, Dodd recognized that "Simmer Down" and the Wailers were exactly what he had been seeking. With their eternal screwfaces—"We were frowny, frowny people," Peter Tosh conceded about that time—and rude-boy aura, the group had the necessary "street" credibility. And as one of the first Jamaican songs to capture the situation in the Kingston ghetto in the language—musically and lyrically—of the ghetto dwellers themselves, "Simmer Down" was the perfect vehicle to use to introduce the group to the public.

A SIMMERING HIT

"Simmer Down" reached the top of the Jamaican charts in February 1964 and spent several months blaring from seemingly every West Kingston barroom jukebox. Though the song urged the rude boys to temper their violent ways, it also clearly implied that the Wailers understood their anger and frustration and were, in fact, on their side. "Simmer down," the Wailers sang, their own voices seething, "the battle will get hotter." Hold your anger, that is, until the time is right. The music was pure, relentless ska, the rude boys' own hopped-up rhythm of choice, clearly identifying the Wailers, in the popular mind, as incipient street rebels. As the Trench Town denizens immediately realized, this was music made by the have-nots for the have-nots.

That image was solidified by the various hits the Wailers recorded with the Skatalites for Dodd over the next several years, including "Rude Boy," "Rule Dem Rude," "Steppin' Razor," and "Jailhouse." During that time, the group also became almost as well known for its love songs, like "I Need You So" and Marley's achingly beautiful "It Hurts to Be Alone," which displayed the soft side that those who got beyond the screwface always found so endearing.

Also, the band covered American songs, like Marley's rewrite of his beloved Drifters' "On Broadway" and the group's version of Aaron Neville's "Ten Commandments of Love," not to mention more unlikely remakes, like Burt Bacharach's "What's New, Pussycat?" and Irving Berlin's "White Christmas." If such songs seemed odd material for the rebellious Wailers, as incongruous as the gold lamé suits that Dodd

Clement Dodd, shown here in 2002, was a mentor to Bob Marley and the other Wailers in the early 1960s. The group auditioned for Dodd, known as "Sir Coxsone," under a mango tree behind his Trench Town production facility, Studio One. The Wailers' vocal sophistication and seriousness impressed Dodd.

dressed them in for their many appearances, the Wailers themselves were not greatly bothered by any possible contradiction. "Knowing that we found reality and righteousness, we relaxed," Tosh said. "So when you saw us in the slick suits and things, we were just in the thing that was looked on as the thing at the time. So we just adjusted ourselves materially."

Gold lamé could not hide the group's originality. "They have a different sense of music," explained Alton Ellis, whose recordings often competed with the Wailers' on the Jamaican charts, "and we all love it.... Bob's sound was always different: It mesmerized me from those times. His music always have a roots sense of direction. Not even just the words—I'm talking about the melody that him sing, the feel of the rhythm. Always a bit different." Paradoxically, the spontaneity and rebelliousness that Ellis and others responded to in the Wailers' music was made possible only by intense preparation and endless rehearsal: Their complete mastery of the material allowed the Wailers to express it with perfect freedom. That dedication, in turn, was only possible through a mutual friendship as tight as the group's harmonies. As Johnny Moore of the Skatalites observed, "At the time, they were very young and vibrant and you could see they were very good friends: they were very, very close to one another. They really did care about each other. I guess that's why they made a success of it as it was."

For all the musical benefits of the Wailers' association with Dodd, the relationship was destined to be short-lived. After their initial audition, Dodd had signed them on his usual terms—a flat fee of 15 pounds (about $60) per record, with no royalties. As newcomers to the recording game, with no clout in the industry, the Wailers had no choice but to agree. Dodd's subsequent decision to put the group on a weekly salary of three pounds did little to ease their discontent; for that money, they found, they were expected to be on almost permanent call at Studio One, available around the clock to record backing vocals on other tracks Dodd was producing, or to coach, rehearse, and prepare other groups. If their inquiries about royalties or more equitable arrangements grew too strident, Dodd referred them to the pistol he kept in his studio as the ultimate answer to such ingratitude.

Of the three Wailers, Marley was perhaps the most distressed by the group's relationship with Dodd. The producer liked to tell people that he had "adopted" the Wailers, and he had, in fact, given Marley a home of sorts, a spare room in a shack behind the studio where the musician slept on an unhinged wooden door laid on two cinder blocks. The musical education he was getting at Studio One was priceless, too; constant proximity to Ernest Ranglin had improved Marley's guitar playing, and he was being exposed to all kinds of intriguing new sounds that were expanding his own musical creativity. These new sounds included those of the Beatles and Bob Dylan; Marley would even rework Dylan's classic "Like a Rolling Stone" for the Wailers. Yet there was certainly something wrong when the leader of the hottest group in Jamaican music—at one point in 1965, records by the Wailers occupied positions one, two, three, seven, and nine on the Jamaican charts—was living penniless in a donated shack.

MARLEY IN LOVE

Complicating the situation by the end of 1965 was Marley's relationship with Alvarita Anderson, an aspiring nurse and teacher who also taught Sunday school and sang with her own Motown-inspired group, the Soulettes. The dirt path the Wailers walked each day to Studio One wound right behind the house where Anderson lived with her aunt, and like others in Trench Town she was fascinated by these boys who "sounded like angels" but looked to her, as she watched them pass by every day, "like rough little guys." (At six feet, Tosh was by far the tallest of the Wailers; Marley was, at most, five-foot-eight, and Livingston was several inches shorter than that.) Anderson, known to everyone as Rita,

Like Bob Marley, Peter Tosh saw music as a way out of Trench Town. Shown here in the 1980s in the midst of his solo career, Tosh had a personality that was as charming and outgoing as it was sometimes menacing.

was too shy to introduce herself, but in time a friend arranged for the Soulettes to audition for Dodd, and she reminded the Wailers, who were present at the time, that she was the girl they saw each day as they went to work.

Impressed by the Soulettes, Dodd agreed to record them, and he assigned Marley to be their "manager"—that is, to rehearse them and prepare them for their professional debut. The decision did not make Anderson especially happy, as she later recalled:

> Bob was very strange from them times. He didn't talk much, and he didn't laugh much. He was more observing. Also, he would lead the rehearsals, and we were

Rita Marley

Rita Marley's life has been filled with the highs of having musical success and a family that continually surrounded her, and the lows of feeling alone and unhappy.

Yet, since her husband's death in 1981, Rita Marley has made sure that the world continues to remember the music of Bob Marley. She has also provided support to his 12 children—the 5 children who are her own and the 7 others that Bob Marley fathered with other women during their marriage. (After Bob's death, Rita had another child, named Serita, whose father is her longtime friend, Owen Stewart.)

The young Alvarita Anderson was only five years old when her mother left her, her brother, and their father to be with another man. For a while, Rita bounced back and forth between the homes of her mother and her grandmother. But her father eventually found this ridiculous and persuaded his childless sister to help him take care of his children in his own home.

Rita's Aunt Viola, whom she called Aunty, was the light in her life, and Rita grew up under Aunty's loving guidance. The Anderson family was a musical group, and every evening the family gathered to sing under the plum tree in their yard. Rita's relatives sang in church choirs and at weddings and other celebrations. Aunty recognized Rita's musical talents and, when Rita was 10, she encouraged her to try out for a local radio show called *Opportunity Knocks*. When Rita won the contest on the program, she began taking herself seriously as a singer. Encouraged in her ambitions by her Aunt Viola—Rita's very scared of him because of the discipline he would put on his rehearsals and the type of harmony that we sing. So he wasn't a favorite of ours at that time. We used to think that this man is very cross. Nothing but music. No girls, no anything. He was totally different.... He was very firm about what we were about: if you come to the studio, you don't come to play; you're here to work. As long as Marley was there, that discipline was established.

father lived in England for 10 years while she was growing up—Rita continued her musical pursuits into her teen years, singing for fun with a male cousin and a good friend.

Rita's plan was to be a nurse and she was trained to do that, but before she could begin a job she became pregnant by a boy she was dating. She gave birth to her first child, Sharon, but never married the baby's father. Sharon was not even a year old when Rita met a Trench Town band called the Wailers, whose members walked by her house nearly every day. Rita and two female friends auditioned at the Wailers' studio, and they became the Soulettes, the back-up group for the Wailers. The Wailers' shy guitarist, whom Rita knew as Robbie, soon became the love of her life. After their wedding, Sharon was officially adopted by her new father.

For many years, Rita Marley hardly had the time to pursue a musical career—she cared for her children and sometimes worked as a nurse or as household help to supplement the family's income. Later, she became part of Marley's back-up group, known as the I-Threes, and was on tour with him when his cancer was diagnosed. Since her husband's death, Rita has added several solo singles and albums to her name. In 1991 her fourth album, *We Must Carry On*, was nominated for a Grammy. She has bought a home in Ghana, Africa, and has plans to build a recording studio there. And, she helps support her grandchildren—numbering at least 38—with the proceeds from the sales of Bob Marley records.

She was thus stunned when, after several weeks, Livingston told her that Marley was in love with her. Even with his secret revealed, Marley found it hard to speak of his feelings directly; he preferred to write love letters, which Livingston would deliver. Though she was initially attracted to Tosh, who could be as outgoing and charming as he was sometimes menacing, Anderson began to look at Marley differently. "You have to be prepared to meet him," she explained. "Then when you do, you find that behind all of that he is the nicest person, like an angel."

His developing relationship with Anderson gave Marley one more reason for wanting a more settled existence. Even before the two became a couple, he was growing desperate to escape the barren quarters Dodd had given him. His seriousness and air of withdrawal were more than just temperament, Anderson learned; he was literally haunted. One day, he confided in her that he got almost no sleep at night and felt his strength was being gradually drained from his body: A duppy had been set upon him and did its evil work each night in the shack behind Studio One. Anderson was extremely skeptical, but when she spent one night with Marley in the room she was awakened from sleep by a terrifying sensation that "felt as though someone came into the room and held me down. You'd try to get out of this grip and feel as though you were going into a trance; you couldn't speak; you couldn't talk; you couldn't see anything—you just felt the sensation." Frightened into belief, she brought Marley home to the house where she lived with her aunt, who, when she realized how serious the couple were about their relationship, agreed to build a little shack for them.

A short time later, on February 10, 1966, Bob Marley and Rita Anderson were formally married. The ceremony did not mean that their life together was settled in any meaningful way, however, for on the very next day Bob left—alone—for the United States. Discouraged by the Jamaican music business, he knew he had to find another way, and he hoped to find some answers in the States.

5

The Rasta Influence

Bob Marley returned to Kingston in October 1966, bringing with him the first electric guitar he ever owned and $700 to start a record company. Just a day after his marriage to Rita, Bob had left Kingston to join his mother in Delaware to try to sort out his life. There, he held a succession of odd jobs—working as a laboratory assistant, washing dishes in a restaurant, driving a forklift in a factory, and manning the assembly line in a Chrysler automobile plant—while laying his plans. Now, he was back in Kingston and ready to push ahead.

Musical success had not translated into financial reward for the Wailers; if the group was to control its own destiny, it needed financial as well as artistic independence. Accordingly, Marley planned to use the money he made in the United States—a large sum by Jamaican standards—to start his own record label, enabling the Wailers to break free of Dodd. His return to Jamaica came at a time when dramatic changes were occurring that would affect the Wailers and their music. During the short time he was gone, a monumental event had occurred: In April 1966, Emperor Haile Selassie I of Ethiopia visited Jamaica.

For the island's Rastas, Selassie's arrival represented much more than the stopover of a foreign dignitary on a state visit. It was nothing less than the incarnation of the Messiah on Jamaican soil. For the ever-growing number of Rastas, Selassie's crowning as emperor of Ethiopia in 1930 had fulfilled biblical prophecy, most notably as expressed in the fifth chapter of Revelation, which discusses "the Lion of the tribe of Judah."

Selassie's given name, Ras Tafari Makonnen, was adopted as the name—Rastafari—by which the new religion became known. That religion drew on a long tradition of black Jamaicans thinking that Ethiopia was the lost homeland and promised holy land of an exiled people—beliefs that held obvious appeal for a people acutely aware of their slave heritage. Rastas believe their religion to be the pure and uncorrupted culmination of Judeo-Christian traditions, as maintained over the years in the Ethiopian Orthodox Church.

As any Rasta knows, it takes three and a half years, at the rate of a single chapter each day, to read the Bible from Genesis to Revelation, and few of the genuine believers have not completed this task. They apply their own interpretation to its words, however, and regard the existing Christian churches as corrupt agents of a social system that operates to oppress blacks. Rastas metaphorically liken their situation in Jamaica to the captivity of the Old Testament Jews in Babylon. (In the New Testament, Babylon is also the name of the great earthly city in the Book of Revelation that is made "desolate" for its sinfulness.) Jamaica is thus literally regarded as hell on earth; Ethiopia is the lost promised land to which the faithful aspire to return; and Zion (a biblical name for the kingdom of Israel) is the eternal land of redemption and rest awaiting the faithful

DID YOU KNOW?

Bob Marley's religion, Rastafari, affected his hairstyle and his lifestyle. Marley's renowned dreadlocks were grown in response to his dedication to the Rastafarian faith, which prohibits the combing or cutting of hair. Rastas also use only natural substances to wash their hair, never resorting to chemically prepared shampoos and products. Marley tried to grow dreadlocks a few times, including once in 1968, but he cut them at the insistence of his mother, whom he was visiting in the United States. Finally, in 1972, Marley committed to growing the dreadlocks for which he later acquired much fame. Named for the dread that they conjured up in non-Rastas because of their unkempt look, the popularity of dreadlocks has grown through the decades.

Also as a Rastafarian, Marley was a proponent for the legalization of marijuana. Rastafarians believe that marijuana should be used as a sacrament and as an aid to meditation. Rasta leaders encourage the smoking of marijuana as a religious rite and cite discussions of its use in biblical psalms. For the Rasta, marijuana is a natural instrument of meditation given by Jah (the Supreme Being of Rastafari) to his people. They cite numerous biblical passages that seem to sanction its use, such as Psalms 104:14: "He causeth the grass to grow for the cattle, and herb for the service of man: that he may bring forth food out of the earth."

at the end of one's temporal life on earth. Babylon, for the Rasta, is this temporal existence, in all its entirety and individual facets, as well as all those workings and manifestations of society that keep "I and I" (as the Rasta refers to himself and the rest of the brethren) "downpressed."

Rastas seek as little contact with the system, with Babylon, as possible. Many refuse to vote, pay taxes, send their children to school, or otherwise engage with society. In the early days of the movement, from the 1930s through the 1950s, as it gained adherents among the impoverished elements of Jamaican society, Rastas lived close to nature in encampments in the hills of eastern Jamaica or on the less-frequented beaches, making a subsistence living as small farmers, artists and craftsmen, or fishermen.

Strictly adhering to a diet they consider *ital*—pure, unprocessed, clean—they eat mostly grains, fruits, vegetables, and fish, and forbid the consumption of meat and shellfish; likewise, beverages are restricted to products that come directly from the earth: water, juices, and herbal teas, but not milk or coffee. Rastas disdain the use of most seasonings, like salt, and prohibit tobacco and alcohol use, which they see as a destructive force that has been pushed on blacks by whites. "Rum mosh up your insides," Marley explained, "Just kill ya, like the system."

The opposition of the authorities and the disdain of most elements of Jamaican society did not slow the growth of Rastafari. When Haile Selassie's plane touched down in Kingston on April 21, 1966, more than 100,000 of the brethren awaited him on the tarmac. The size and intensity of the gathering startled the emperor no less than it did the Jamaican government; initially, an overwhelmed Selassie could not be persuaded to leave his jet, and he wept when he emerged. The reception accorded the emperor also alerted the government that this grassroots, hill-country religion was not, as they had long hoped, dying out. The government soon mounted one of its periodic crackdowns on the Rastas, culminating in the bulldozing of the Back O' the Wall shantytown, with its many Rasta enclaves, in the summer of 1966. The destruction only confirmed what the Rastas believed about the nature of Babylon.

Despite Rita Marley's upbringing in the church, she had come to mistrust the common characterization of the Rastas as dangerous and violent; she was moved by their poverty, their dignity, their humility, and the simple beauty of their call for "One Love" to unite all people. On April 21, she was among the huge throng of Jamaicans—even more than gathered at the airport—who lined the streets of Kingston as Haile

Haile Selassie, the emperor of Ethiopia from 1930 to 1974, was regarded as a messiah by the Rastafarians. When he visited Jamaica in 1966, more than 100,000 people turned out to meet him on the airport's tarmac. After Rita Marley saw Haile Selassie pass in his motorcade, she was moved to convert to the Rastafarian religion.

H.I.M. Haile Selassie I

Since the mid-1700s, many Jamaicans have seen Ethiopia as their African home. In 1930, Ras Tafari Makonnen, the great-grandson of King Saheka Selassie of Showa, became the emperor of Ethiopia. Makonnen then took the name of His Imperial Majesty Haile Selassie I. He was considered the 225th king in a direct line of descent from the biblical King Solomon and the Queen of Sheba. At the time of his coronation, poor Jamaicans saw him as the fulfillment of a prophecy; thus began the Rastafarian religion.

Selassie himself was never a member of the Rastafari faith, and he did not believe the divine claims the Rastafari made of him. During the 1960s and 1970s, he worked for pan-African issues, mainly through the Organization of African Unity. On October 4, 1963, Selassie addressed the United Nations about important issues of the time: disarmament and the establishment of true equality for all. The following is an excerpt of his speech, summing up his dedication to peace:

> The preservation of peace and the guaranteeing of man's basic freedoms and rights require courage and eternal vigilance, that the least transgression of international morality shall not go undetected and unremedied. These lessons must be learned anew by each succeeding generation, and that generation is fortunate indeed which learns from other than its own bitter experience. This organization and each of its members bear a crushing and awesome responsibility: to absorb the wisdom of history and to apply it to the problems of the present, in order that future generations may be born, and live, and die, in peace.

Selassie continued to rule Ethiopia into the 1970s, until the army seized control of the country in 1974. Selassie was gradually stripped of his powers, and he was deposed on September 12, 1974. A year later, he was killed in prison by order of the coup leaders.

Selassie's motorcade passed through. With a clear view of the emperor's limousine, she cautiously told herself that she would await a sign of his divinity. As she caught her first glimpse of the Ethiopian ruler, she was disappointed. He was small and slight: not very impressive. But then he looked directly at Rita and waved, and she has said she saw stigmata—the wounds of the crucified Christ—in the palm of his hands. Her conversion to the Rastafarian lifestyle was virtually immediate, and she wrote to her husband about the moving experience.

More than any single event, Marley's embrace of Rastafari brought about the full flowering of his artistry, helping him order his understanding of his individual identity, the nature of Jamaican society, and perhaps even the very meaning of earthly existence.

IN THE BUSINESS

The other Wailers were equally drawn to Rastafari, and the three friends began growing their hair out and living according to Rasta tenets. Using the money Marley had earned in Delaware, they established the Wail'N Soul'M record store and label (later just Wail'N Soul or sometimes Wailing Souls), named in honor of its two acts, the Wailers and the Soulettes. Ska was no longer the sound of Jamaica; the new music was rock steady, a slower, less frantic rhythm with a more pronounced bass line that suited the Wailers just fine. Though they recorded some first-rate sides for Wail'N Soul—"Nice Time," "Thank You Lord," "Hypocrites," and "Pyaka," for example— having their own record label proved no guarantee of financial success. The business of distributing the records—usually Rita but sometimes Bob, carried them around town to stores, radio stations, and bars by bicycle—proved exhausting, and the label seldom had enough cash on hand to press enough records to keep up with demand. As a result, the group's popularity once again far exceeded its earnings, as the increased political and social directness of their songs' lyrics was finding an extremely receptive audience among the sufferers.

Discouraged, the Marleys even left Kingston for a time to try their hands at farming the land that Bob's grandfather, Omeriah Malcolm, had left him in Nine Mile. Though the country life was difficult, it put Marley in touch with his roots. Rita, who had spent her entire life in Kingston, said:

It was different. I had to carry water, collect wood to make the fire, and I had to sleep on a little, small bed on the dirt because they didn't have flooring. But it was all out of love—I had decided to do so, and it didn't matter. I was going into the faith of Rastafari, and I was seeking to find an independent sort of self. Because Bob was already exposed to this lifestyle, it was a thrill for him to see me just living it. It was something he had decided he would do eventually—just be a farmer and stay in the country and live. So this was always his feeling: his need to go back into the open country, and just be himself.

This more natural way of life reinforced Marley's newfound faith, and it opened a wellspring of creativity in him. Many of the songs he would record in the next few years—some of his most powerful and well-known works, like "Stir It Up" and "Trench Town Rock"—had their genesis during this retreat to the countryside. Before their return to Kingston in 1970, Bob and Rita were blessed with the birth of two children, daughter Cedella and son David (known as Ziggy), and Bob adopted Rita's daughter from a previous relationship, Sharon.

PRODUCER TO PRODUCER

The music business, though, remained a struggle. At different times, Livingston and Tosh were arrested for marijuana possession and had to serve fairly lengthy sentences, preventing the group from working together. Wail'N Soul went bust, forcing the Wailers to hustle up new arrangements. They made a deal with Johnny Nash, a moderately successful black American singer who had become fascinated by Jamaican music. Nash had been introduced to Marley at a Rasta gathering, where Marley played one extraordinary song after another on his acoustic guitar. Nash and his manager, Danny Sims, immediately arranged to sign Marley to their publishing company as a songwriter and to place the Wailers on retainer to make demo records for them. The arrangement provided the Wailers with some badly needed income, but it did little to further their career and limited some of their creativity.

Desperate, the group even turned to Marley's old nemesis, Leslie Kong. To that point, the only full-length albums released in Jamaica were simply collections of singles. As a "pep talk" to themselves, the Wailers had composed and recorded a cycle of new songs that were related by theme and reflected their religious and political concerns. They wanted Kong to release the material as a true album, just as other important contemporary performers, most notably the Beatles and Bob Dylan, did with their own music. Kong dismissed their concerns and insisted on releasing the work as *The Best of the Wailers*. An angry Bunny Livingston echoed Marley's earlier prediction to the producer: "How can you know the best of someone's work, when we have such a long trod ahead of us? If this is our best to you, it must mean that you are at the end of your life." Kong released the album as he had planned. Less than a week later, he dropped dead of a heart attack, at age 38, and Livingston's statement, as well as Marley's earlier warning, was frequently recalled.

Marley foresaw an early death for himself as well, offering a possible explanation for the almost frightening sense of urgency he brought to his music and career. In mid-1969, he was in Wilmington, having returned there to earn some money on the assembly line at Chrysler. He often thought wistfully of Jamaica and the Wailers. One day a friend tried to console him, assuring him that he had a long life ahead in which to produce music. "No, mon," Marley told him quite seriously, "me know I going to die when 36."

He was back in Kingston by the end of the year. A musician who worked with the Wailers around that time remembered the mood being constantly somber, urgent, "always screwface," as he put it. The dread aspect the Wailers were taking on as a result of their embrace of Rastafari and incidents like the one with Kong did little to ease their way in the music business. Producers preferred to work with musicians who asked fewer questions and were less likely to stand up for their rights.

A NEW COLLABORATION

Lee Perry, however, was not afraid of the Wailers. Perry was known as "Scratch." "My name is Scratch, from the beginning, and everybody have to start from scratch," he explained. "Anyone deny that, him fall." The diminutive, talkative producer was carving out a reputation as one of Jamaica's greatest musical artists. Most important, he was being credited with almost single-handedly inventing Jamaica's new sound, a mystifyingly hypnotic music called reggae, which featured a beat even slower than rock steady—one that made you feel, Scratch said, "like you stepping in glue." Though the origin of the word is unknown, its practitioners were sure of its meaning. "Reggae means coming from the people, you know?" explained lead singer Toots Hibbert of Toots and the Maytals, one of the few Jamaican groups that can rightfully consider themselves the Wailers' peers. "Reggae mean *regular* people who are suffering, and don't have what they want."

Perry's collaboration with the Wailers seemed natural. Like them, he had served his time—as a DJ and a producer—with Clement Dodd and had left feeling criminally underpaid. Determined, he said, "to upset" the Jamaican music scene with his new sound, he had in his employ the island's foremost instrumental group, after the demise of the original Skatalites in 1965. Membership in the Hippy Boys or Upsetters, as the band variously billed itself, alternated around the group's two founders and rhythm section, bassist Aston "Family Man" Barrett and, on drums, Aston's younger brother, Carlton Barrett. As fellow Rastas and musicians, the Barretts had long wanted to hook up with the Wailers. "We have a special respect and love for the Wailers, and the whole concept of them," Family Man said. "It was good energy coming from the beginning....

When the Wailers hooked up with producer Lee "Scratch" Perry, they added the brothers Aston "Family Man" Barrett and Carlton Barrett. With Aston Barrett's instrumental support, the Wailers took on the sound for which they are best known. Many fans regard these recordings as the Wailers' greatest.

The Wailers was the best vocal group, and I group was the best little backing band at the time, so we say why don't we just come together and smash the world?"

With the Barretts' band, the Wailers worked with Perry through late 1969 and most of 1970. It was a nearly perfect artistic collaboration. With its simmering, percolating beats, reggae is bass-driven music above all, and in Family Man the

Wailers had one of the world's best guitarists (as attested to by no less a musical authority than Miles Davis, the peerless American jazz trumpeter). Family Man was an unusually melodic player who was also a thunderous rhythmic force. Carlton Barrett was almost as inspired a player. Despite personal differences, Perry and Marley immediately established an artistic relationship so close that it was difficult to see, musically, where one left off and the other began.

Counting on Aston Barrett to oversee the instrumentals, Marley began referring to Family Man as his "melodic superintendent," and with his instrumental support the Wailers took on the sound for which they are best known. Without ska's frantic pace, horns, and instrumentation, there was much more space in this music, even more than rock steady had allowed Marley. The Wailers' vocal harmonies became less studied, rougher, more natural, less consciously imitative of American vocal groups. For Marley, the music was endlessly open, receptive to all kinds of influence and experimentation, including American-style rhythm and blues and doo-wop, church-style backing vocals, tinges of rock guitar, burru drumming, even modern jazz. This openness allowed him to combine his talent for buoyant, infectious melodies with lyrics that displayed a genuine gift for simple yet poetic language, mixing Rastafarian, biblical, and folk wisdom with homespun metaphors, distilled observation, and ever-more-direct social and political criticism.

Though less widely distributed than his later work, and thus less well known, the early recordings that Marley and the Wailers made with Perry are regarded by many devotees as their best. Many would become staples of Marley and the Wailers' song catalog and live performances: "Small Axe," "Duppy Conqueror," "Lively Up Yourself," "Kaya," and Tosh's "400 Years." In them, Marley proudly proclaimed that a new day had come; armed with the power of Rastafari, the sufferers could be made free. Jail could not hold them, nor even the power of the dead, as he explained in "Duppy Conqueror": "The bars could not hold me / Force could not control me, now / They try to keep me down / But Jah put I around ... I'm a duppy conqueror."

But there were still some problems that the Wailers could not overcome. Perry packaged the sides the group had recorded for him as three albums—*Soul Rebels*, *Soul Revolution* (sold in some markets as *Rasta Revolution*), and *African Herbsman*—that he sold for distribution in Great Britain and the United States, where large Jamaican immigrant communities created a market. Unfortunately, as Bunny Livingston explained, "We have never made one dime from any of them. Perry refused to give us our money when it came time for us to collect. He said he had decided to just give us some royalties. But we have never seen anything at all. Nothing. Not one penny." When Perry behaved similarly regarding royalties from the Jamaican sales of the records, particularly "Duppy Conqueror," Marley, Livingston, and Tosh, with little other recourse, beat him up. A fellow musician teased them, implying that the crazy dreads had only gotten what they deserved: "Hey, only a Rastaman dare sing about duppy." Though Marley would work with Perry again on occasion, the partnership was broken.

On the brink of greater stardom, the Wailers again turned to the alternative of establishing their own label. Their production company, Tuff Gong, was split in an almost equal three-way partnership among the original Wailers, with Marley holding the slight majority share. Besides financing the start-up cost of the venture, Alan "Skill" Cole, a close friend of Marley's and Jamaica's greatest soccer star, stayed on with the Wailers in an unofficial yet most important capacity. Counteracting the long-time payoff arrangements between the larger labels and the handful of Jamaican radio stations, Cole applied the necessary muscle to get air time for the Wailers. Cole said:

> We have to go up there and have to beat boy. We go and
> fight a system where they just have money power. We

are on the street; we are street boy. We beat program director, disc jockey. Conk them up in them head and kick them batty. They was fighting us because we was Rastas. Bob Marley was the singer; he was a quiet little brethren. Can't do nothing more than be quiet and give you the best lyrics and the best music. So me just deal with things the right and proper way.

Cole's muscle, however, was not necessary to help the first release on Tuff Gong in 1971. "One good thing about music: when it hits, you feel no pain," Marley wrote and sang on "Trench Town Rock," and the sufferers clearly agreed with him. The song topped the Jamaican charts for five months. For Bunny Livingston, "Trench Town Rock" represented the Wailers' true breakthrough, "the tune that made us *really* start to search." Peter Tosh confirmed, "We were now gone into a twelfth dimension."

THE WORLD DISCOVERS REGGAE

As the Wailers were catching fire in Jamaica, reggae was breaking through on the international scene. Johnny Nash's reggae-tinged blockbuster album *I Can See Clearly Now*, featuring four songs written by Marley, went to number one on charts around the world, including the United States. Barbra Streisand was among the many singers who covered at least one of the Marley compositions from the album—in this case, "Guava Jelly." In the wake of the album's success, Nash's manager, Danny Sims, arranged for Marley to go to Stockholm, Sweden, to work on songs for the soundtrack of a planned film starring Nash.

A short time later, a low-budget movie filmed in Kingston, starring Jimmy Cliff as a talented young musician driven by ghetto life and the greed of the music industry to become an outlaw, was released in the United States. *The Harder They Come* became one of the longest-running and highest-grossing cult films in U.S. history. Its epic reggae soundtrack, featuring tunes by a number of the Wailers' contemporaries, did equally well. While Nash's versions were watered-down, homogenized reggae suited for American pop radio and devoid of political content, *The Harder They Come* was the real thing. Reggae was no longer Jamaica's secret, and Kingston was on its way to becoming the "Third World Nashville." Among white rock musicians, like Eric Clapton and the Rolling Stones, reggae was soon to become the hippest new sound.

Only one step remained to complete this transformation. From Stockholm, where the cold Scandinavian weather made for an unpleasant stay, Marley was sent by Sims to London, England. The movie had fallen through, but he was to be joined there by the other Wailers, to back Nash on a concert

Reggae musician Jimmy Cliff (center) was the star of the 1972 movie *The Harder They Come*. The film became a cult classic in the United States. After its release, the audience for reggae broadened beyond Jamaica.

tour. As with many of Sims's ventures, however, this too fell apart, and after just one gig, the Wailers found themselves stranded in cold, rainy England without enough money for return tickets home. To make matters worse, the group members got busted for a package of marijuana sent to their London address by some Kingston friends.

6

Free to Sing

Despite all of the frustrations he was experiencing as he tried to popularize the Wailers and their music, Bob Marley did not give up. He went to see Chris Blackwell, the founder and head of Island, England's largest and most successful independent record company. It was after meeting with Blackwell that Marley and the Wailers finally had license to focus on their creativity, rather than their poor financial status. To everyone's surprise, Blackwell advanced the Wailers the equivalent of about $20,000 to return to Jamaica and record a true album. He then spent another large sum of money to buy the Wailers out of their arrangement with Sims. He even allowed Tuff Gong to maintain the right to distribute the group's material in Jamaica. At last, the Wailers had a record agreement that promised to be creatively and financially profitable to them.

Many people in the music industry thought Blackwell had taken leave of his senses to gamble on a group of reggae artists. To date, no individual reggae artist or group had demonstrated the ability to sell an album in the British and American markets, which is where Blackwell intended to "break" the Wailers. Moreover, of all the Jamaican acts he could have chosen, the Wailers had the reputation of being the most difficult. Blackwell's advisors and other musicians told him to kiss the money good-bye, that "those crazy Rastas" would return to Jamaica and that would be the last he would ever hear from them.

But Blackwell had very good reasons for his actions. A member of a prosperous Anglo-Jamaican family, Blackwell had spent much of his childhood in Jamaica and revered its culture and music. As a teenager, he had developed enormous respect for Rastas when they came to his assistance after a boating accident left him hurt and stranded on a remote part of the island. He perceptively understood that Marley's Rasta beliefs and political convictions were essential to his greatness as an artist—and even purely from a marketing standpoint, he regarded them as a help rather than a hindrance.

To Blackwell, Marley was the real-life counterpart of the character Jimmy Cliff played in *The Harder They Come,* a "rebel-type character" perfect for the rock music market. The record executive savvily recognized that "what Bob Marley believed in and how he lived his life was something that had tremendous appeal for the media.... Now here was this Third World superstar who had a different point of view, an individual against the system, who also had an incredible look: this was the first time you had seen anyone looking like that, other than Jimi Hendrix. And Bob had that power about him, and incredible lyrics." Given all this, Marley's reputation as "trouble," in Blackwell's words, bothered him not a bit: "In my experience when people are described like that, it usually just means that they know what they want."

CATCH A FIRE

The first true reggae album, *Catch a Fire*, was released in Great Britain in December 1972 and in the United States soon after. Though not initially an enormous seller, the album justified Blackwell's faith in the Wailers, garnering lavish praise from critics in Great Britain and the United States. If some listeners in those countries were puzzled by this new Jamaican music, the sufferers had no trouble understanding the references in such songs as "Slave Driver," "400 Years," and "Concrete Jungle." Jamaican poet Linton Kwesi Johnson described *Catch a Fire* as a landmark: "A whole new style of Jamaican music has come into being. It has a different character, a different sound ... what I can only describe as 'International Reggae.' It incorporates elements from popular music internationally: rock and soul, blues and funk."

To support the album, the Wailers toured Great Britain and the United States, another first for a reggae group. Though in the recent past they had only infrequently played live in Jamaica, years of rehearsing and recording together had made the Wailers a precise live act, able to live up to the underground word of mouth that preceded them. At the Speakeasy Club in London, the aristocracy of the British rock world—Mick Jagger, Traffic, Bryan Ferry—turned out for the Wailers' sets and were not disappointed. "Bob had such charisma," said Mick Cater, who was assigned by Island to help the group with its travel arrangements. "He was the best live act there's ever been, both with Peter and Bunny and later without them. A complete powerhouse onstage, but off, nothing like that, just very quiet."

But the warm reception the Wailers received was not sufficient to hide new tensions within the group. The unfamiliar grind of one-night stands in strange cities was especially wearing on Livingston, who was always unhappy anywhere but in Jamaica and often went days without eating when he could not get unprocessed food. Tosh, meanwhile, was growing uncomfortable with what he regarded as an increasing emphasis on Marley as the star, leader, and virtually sole songwriter of the group, which he believed was part of a conscious plan by Marley and Blackwell. Livingston and Tosh stayed on to record the group's second album, the uncompromising *Burnin'*, in early 1973, but that June, Livingston announced he would not be part of the summer tour in the United States. (As a solo artist, he changed his name to Bunny Wailer.) His place was taken by

Peter Tosh

Peter Tosh, one of the original members of the Wailers, is considered a founding father of reggae. Tosh grew up in Trench Town, just a few blocks from Bob Marley's home. As a teenager, Tosh joined Marley and his friend, Bunny Livingston, to form the Wailers. In the beginning, the tall Peter Tosh told people he was the leader of the group and, like Marley, he saw music as his only way out of Trench Town. Although the group's other members were very serious about their future, Tosh seemed even more serious.

It wasn't long after the Wailers became a success that Tosh struck out on his own. Tosh disagreed with music producer Chris Blackwell over finances and, when Blackwell's Island Records refused to pick up his solo album, he quit the Wailers. With the help of Eric Clapton—who made the Wailers' "I Shot the Sheriff" a huge hit—and a network of others, Tosh recorded some of his first tapes at CBS Studios in New York City. In 1975, his songs "Watcha Gonna Do," "Can't Blame the Youth," and "Legalize It"—recorded after a particularly harrowing police arrest for marijuana possession—were all banned from Jamaican radio stations. Meanwhile, all copies sold out: "Legalize It" is still one of Jamaica's top-selling singles.

Tosh released five solo albums from 1976 to 1981. In 1981, his *Wanted Dread and Alive* album climbed to No. 91 on *Billboard* magazine's pop charts. His next album, *Mama Africa* from 1983, went to No. 59. Tosh's outspoken support for the legalization of marijuana continued to cause violent run-ins with Jamaican authorities, causing the musician to retreat to Africa in the early 1980s. Tosh released other well-received albums—including his last, *No Nuclear War*—before his death at age 42 in 1987, when he was killed by unknown assailants in his home in Jamaica.

Joe Higgs, and the Wailers played to enormous acclaim in various clubs in the Northeast, including Max's Kansas City in New York, where they opened for an up-and-coming singer named Bruce Springsteen.

By that time, *Burnin'* had been released. The album featured reworkings of old Wailers material like "Small Axe" and "Duppy Conqueror" as well as new songs: immediate classics like "I Shot the Sheriff," "Burnin' and Lootin'," and "Rastaman Chant," an actual Rasta prayer sung to the accompaniment of burru drums. *Burnin'* was immediately hailed as a reggae masterpiece. It marked the end of the original Wailers, however. During the British club tour that followed at the end of 1973, the increasingly disgruntled Tosh left the group. Alluding to the Wailers' notorious dislike for cold weather, Island explained the cancellation of the remaining dates of the tour with a simple communiqué: "It snowed."

Though hurt by his friends' defection, Marley was also relieved. He had little stomach for the silent tension and angry outbursts that had characterized the trio's relationship while on the road. Never one to allow anything to interfere with his own creative drive, he was increasingly less willing to compromise to maintain group harmony.

A NEW GROUP

From that point forward, the group would be Bob Marley and the Wailers, with no question as to who was the leader. Marley expanded the group's sound, adding to the Barretts, at various intervals, young keyboard wizards Earl "Wire" Lindo and Tyrone Downie, guitarists Al Anderson and Junior Marvin, his old friend Seeco Patterson on percussion, and the I-Threes— Rita Marley, Marcia Griffiths, and Judy Mowatt—on backing vocals. If reggae purists sometimes decried the rock tinge that the addition of the guitarists brought about, there was no denying that the revamped Wailers constituted an ensemble of unparalleled vocal and instrumental power. "One time I hear

The I-Threes sang backing vocals for Bob Marley and the Wailers. They were (from left) Judy Mowatt, Rita Marley, and Marcia Griffiths. Of the performances, Mowatt said, "It was a clean feeling: you leave a concert as though you have learned something, have gained something."

them say we finish with the tour," Family Man remembered about the troubles with Tosh and Livingston. "I think, 'Finish with it?' I think the tour just get started."

The new group was first heard on record in late 1974, when *Natty Dread* was released. The record was, in many ways, Marley's most outspoken yet, featuring such melodic, militant, poetic anthems as "Talkin' Blues," "Revolution," "Them Belly Full (But We Hungry)," and "Rebel Music," as well as the haunting, lovely "No Woman, No Cry."

Natty Dread was recorded over several months in 1974 in Jamaica, where Marley, having achieved a certain level of the success that had long eluded him, relaxed into an almost settled way of life, at least for him. While his wife and their four children lived in a modern house in the Rasta enclave at Bull Bay, 10 miles east of Kingston, he spent much of his time at

Island House, the rambling home at 56 Hope Road, in a tony section of Kingston, that Blackwell had sold to him.

LIFE OFF THE STAGE

At Island House, he occupied a small upstairs bedroom, unfurnished and undecorated except for a small mattress, a portrait of Haile Selassie on the wall, and his ever-present guitar. Various Rastas and musicians were always in residence or coming and going from the house, as were one or another of Marley's lovers, who included the acclaimed Jamaican actress Esther Anderson; the women's table tennis champion of the Caribbean, Anita Belnavis; and the stunningly beautiful Cindy Breakespeare, who would be named Miss World in 1976. Sometimes Marley escaped with these companions to various hideaways he had around the island; his grandfather's house at Nine Mile also remained a refuge for him.

This "gypsy" aspect of Marley's personality, as a friend characterized it, was no secret to those close to him, including his wife: "It is something you learn to live with over a period of time," Rita Marley said. "I think Bob had such a lack of love when he was growing up. He seemed to be trying to prove to himself whether someone loved him and how much they loved him. There came a time when I had to say to him, 'If that's what you want, then I'll have to learn to live with it.'" Indeed, Rita opened up her home and helped raise many of the children Marley fathered outside the marriage, all of whom he acknowledged and supported. Although he was not constantly living at Bull Bay, Bob and Rita's daughter Cedella recalled that "he was around," and that "it was kind of strict at home: you came home, you did your homework, and you went to bed."

At 56 Hope Road, Marley maintained a similar kind of discipline. Able to function with very little sleep, he was unfailingly the last one to bed at night—Judy Mowatt remembers that "if you went to Bob's room at midnight, one o'clock, three o'clock, Bob would be playing a song"—and the first awake, usually with the sun. Most mornings, Alan Cole led Marley and company on a training run, a "little eye-opener," as Marley called it, that sometimes stretched out as far as 18 miles. Afterward, if there were no rehearsals or recording sessions scheduled, Marley liked to sit with his guitar on the steps of the back porch, one of his favorite spots for writing songs. Such days were always punctuated with the frequent sacramental intake of marijuana, followed by the freewheeling, imaginative Rasta discussions known as "reasonings." And it was the rare afternoon that passed by without some kind of soccer game, the singer himself being a superb player of virtually professional caliber.

At some point, Marley would meet with the many people who came to the house each day seeking his counsel. They included friends; fellow musicians; gunmen, rudies, and dreads from the ghetto; and poor people looking for help or money. According to Gilly Gilbert, the cook at the house who prepared such ital dishes as green banana porridge and fish head stew, "People come, hungry, and him try for help hungry people and poor people. Some him help, appreciate it, some no appreciate.... He try to help everyone, please everyone." Friends say that Marley sometimes gave away as much as $40,000 at such sessions.

"He gave whatever to whoever. He didn't prize material things. And he didn't prize money. And he would always say that it was just passing through, so it wasn't important.... I think he felt that that was part of his role in life—to do for others and to give to others, and I think he felt very blessed because of the level of inspiration and the work that he had been called to do," said Cindy Breakespeare, who is the mother of Marley's son Damian, aka Junior Gong.

A SUPERSTAR

Despite his lack of interest in being a celebrity, *Natty Dread* catapulted Marley into true international superstardom. The

The release of the album *Natty Dread* propelled Bob Marley to international stardom. His performances were often emotional for those attending. A critic for *The Washington Post* called a concert by Bob Marley and the Wailers "an apocalypse you can dance to."

way had been prepared the previous summer, when Eric Clapton's cover of "I Shot the Sheriff" became a huge hit in Great Britain and the United States. Marley and the "new" Wailers

IN HIS OWN WORDS...

Global unity was the call from Bob Marley throughout his musical career. His song "One Love" has become a simple two-word greeting by people around the world.

> One love, one heart
> Let's get together and feel all right
> Hear the children crying (One love)
> Hear the children crying (One heart)
> Sayin', "Give thanks and praise to the Lord and I will feel all right."
> Sayin', "Let's get together and feel all right."

thus went out on the road in the summer of 1975 to a tumult of acclaim—interviews, magazine covers, sold-out shows at ever-larger venues. The five shows at the Lyceum Ballroom in London were recorded for a concert album, *Live!*, which featured a particularly moving rendition of "No Woman, No Cry" and succeeded in capturing the live power of the "Trench Town experience," the tag with which stage announcers sometimes introduced Marley and the Wailers.

Indeed, the magnitude of the emotions generated by Marley onstage could be overwhelming. A listener at one of Marley's concerts, wrote a critic for *The Washington Post*, "would have thought it was a political rally or a religious revival, not a pop concert ... an apocalypse you can dance to." The first time she saw her son perform, in Philadelphia in 1976, Cedella Marley Booker was inspired to convert to Rastafari. Indeed, Marley and his fellow musicians regarded themselves as missionaries, dedicated to spreading the truth of Jah Rastafari. Judy Mowatt remembered:

It was a crusade, it was a mission. We were like sentinels, like lights. On tour the shows were like church: Bob delivering his sermon. There were mixed emotions in the audience: you see people literally crying, people in a frenzy, on a spiritual high.... There was a power that pulled you there. It was a clean feeling: you leave a concert as though you have learned something, have gained something.

Marley saw himself mainly as a peaceful "soul rebel." "Me only have one ambition," he asserted. "I only have one thing I really like to see happen. I like to see mankind live together—black, white, Chinese, everyone—that's all.... I don't come down on you really with blood and fire, earthquake and lightning, but you must know, see, that within me all that exists, too." Despite the mellow, sinuous melodies, Marley's music expressed some of the anger within, in his calls to "Stir It Up" and "Get Up, Stand Up." "Slave driver, the table is turned / Catch a fire so you can get burned," he sang on "Slave Driver." "Ev'ry time I hear the crack of the whip / My blood runs cold."

GOVERNMENT OPPOSITION

Such messages greatly unsettled the political authorities in Jamaica. The government strongly urged the tourist board and other outlets to play down Jamaica's association with reggae, Rasta, and especially Marley. "We obviously face a contradiction between the message of urban poverty and protest which reggae conveys and that of pleasure and relaxation inherent in our holiday product," read an internal Jamaica Tourist Board memo dated October 10, 1975. "In short, when we promote reggae music we are promoting an aspect of Jamaican culture which is bound to draw attention to some of the harsher circumstances of our lives."

As these circumstances grew harsher, official opposition to Marley intensified. The U.S. Central Intelligence Agency (CIA) designated him for its "most-watched" list in Jamaica, and the American ambassador told the head of his British record label that the U.S. government was not happy about Marley, that "he was capable of destabilizing" the situation in the Caribbean. After the release of *Rastaman Vibration* in 1976, the Jamaican government formally banned four Marley songs from the radio—"War," "Crazy Baldheads," "Who the Cap Fit," and "Rat Race." As Marley became embroiled in the heightened tensions during an election year in Jamaica, his life—like that of many prophets before him—became endangered by those who wished to silence his message of social justice.

In the previous national elections, held in 1972, Marley openly supported the experiment in "democratic socialism" proposed by Michael Manley, the leader of the People's National Party (PNP) and winner of the election. In contrast to the conservative Jamaica Labour Party (JLP) agenda, the PNP's program was more appealing to Marley and other Rastas because of its emphasis on various social programs for the sufferers; its emphasis on socialism as opposed to capitalism as a means of redistributing wealth more fairly among the various levels of Jamaican society; restrictions on foreign exploitation of Jamaican resources; and a foreign policy that moved Jamaica closer toward Cuba and other Caribbean nations (many of them predominantly black) and further from the United States. In addition, Manley reached out to the Rasta community, receiving an audience with Haile Selassie and speaking positively of the Rastas' cultural influence.

By 1976, Marley's Rasta faith had become more militant. Disillusioned by Manley's failure to legalize marijuana and by his creation of special courts that harshly dispensed summary justice to poor blacks, Marley was reluctant to support the PNP for re-election. Nonetheless, he was certainly more inclined toward the PNP, with its slogans of "Power to the People" and "Better Must Come," than he was to Edward Seaga's conservative JLP, which had the backing of the CIA. Specifying several conditions, Marley finally assented to the Manley government's request that he play a concert. The performance on December 5 at the National Heroes Circle Stadium was to be a nonpolitical, nonpartisan event. With the free concert, Marley wished to thank Jamaicans for their support of his musical career, a gesture that he hoped would help bring a year plagued by election-related violence to a peaceful close. The concert would be named after his latest single release, "Smile Jamaica," a lighthearted declaration of his pride in his Jamaican identity.

The Manley government agreed to Marley's conditions, but almost immediately after the singer announced his plans for the concert, the PNP declared that the national elections would be held 15 days later, on December 20. The proximity of the two dates made it appear as if Marley's Smile Jamaica concert was intended to be an endorsement of the PNP. Now Marley began receiving death threats.

As the day of the concert approached, the pressure mounted. A PNP vigilante squad set up a 24-hour armed guard outside Marley's home at 56 Hope Road. The security hardly made Marley, the Wailers, or the I-Threes feel safer as they continued with their daily rehearsals. At this point Marley was nearly as great an irritant to the PNP as he was to the JLP; perhaps the government would not mind if he were out of the way. Perhaps he was being set up; the authorities could always blame the JLP for any harm that came to him.

The constant tension undermined the Wailers' usual musical cohesiveness, and rehearsals proceeded fitfully. By late November, Marcia Griffiths, one of the I-Threes, became so unnerved that she told Marley she could not perform with him and left Jamaica. Another member of the trio, Judy Mowatt, was having ominous recurring dreams, which she interpreted as meaning that something awful was going to happen to Marley. Marley himself was haunted by a shadowy dream in which he was pursued by the sound of "pure gunshot."

ASSASSINS ATTACK

Around nine o'clock on the night of December 3, Marley and the Wailers had just taken a short break from rehearsals.

Marley had stepped into the kitchen to eat a grapefruit. From the porch of 56 Hope Road, percussionist Seeco Patterson noticed, with some concern, that the PNP vigilantes had disappeared. Suddenly, two white cars drove into the compound. Six gunmen exited the vehicles and began firing at the house with automatic weapons. Two of them burst inside, shooting wildly at anything that moved, and then the murderous entourage vanished into the night.

Don Taylor, Marley's manager, took four bullets in the back and was initially pronounced dead at a Kingston hospital before being airlifted to Miami, Florida, for surgery that saved his life. A bullet grazed Rita Marley's skull and knocked her unconscious. Marley was wounded in the chest and left arm. After being treated that night at a Kingston hospital, he retreated to a home in the Blue Mountains owned by Island Records chief Chris Blackwell. There, in seclusion, guarded by a cadre of machete-wielding local Rastas, Marley pondered what to do while rumors about his condition and the identity and motives of his assailants swept the island.

Two days later, Marley was quiet as his escorts drove him down the mountainside. His whereabouts had been a secret, the subject of frenzied speculation. He was wounded; he was unharmed. He was safe; he was dead. He would appear tonight and prophesy for the people; no, he was gone, into exile in England or Florida, on some other island or in some safer place than the tortured paradise of Jamaica.

Sitting with Marley in the backseat of the red Volvo, the police commissioner opened a small briefcase. Removing the components of a submachine gun, he quickly assembled the weapon. The officer in the passenger seat in front did the same, as did those riding in the other vehicles in the swift-moving motorcade. Just in case, the commissioner assured the still-silent prophet, who was now wearing his famous screwface. Marley's message was with that expression: Do not mess with me.

"He would wear a screwface to keep people away," a friend explained. "When you are pure in heart, you can feel when impurity comes near you. The spirits don't mesh." Another friend agreed. "Him only shield he could wear was him noted screwface," this man recalled. It was a means of self-protection familiar to his fellow sufferers, learned from hard times and hard knocks at the hands of the "downpressers." The prophet was "born screw," Rita Marley once said. "Him not have to make it up."

His wife, her own head bandaged where a bullet had grazed her skull, had begged him not to go with these men down the mountain. Marley was still wearing bandages over his bullet wounds. In front, the car's radio crackled. One of Marley's guards spoke into a walkie-talkie, then listened intently and relayed the information to him. The crowd at the National Heroes Circle Stadium in Kingston, their destination, was growing by the minute. Rumors that Marley's appearance had been canceled, even that he was dead, had not discouraged the people. By four o'clock that afternoon, 50,000 spectators had gathered at the stadium. The crowd then swelled to up to 80,000.

Outside the window of the automobile, a gentle Jamaican December night was softly falling as the motorcade wound its way down the mountainside. In the slowly gathering dusk, firelight flickered here and there, leaping upward from rusty metal barrels and stacks of recently gathered scrapwood—the bonfires around which the sufferers gathered to cook, to socialize, to talk, to sing, to remember the other nights they had spent like this, and to remind one another to "no cry." Marley had spent many nights like this, around the fire "with the good people we meet" at the house of his friend, Tartar. With those friends, he had not worn the screwface. Back then he had smiled in his soft way and laughed and sang with them all as his friend Georgie kept the fire burning, until at last he would go to bed, alone on a wood table in a cold corner of a friend's kitchen. He was one of them, the sufferers knew; even death could never take him from them. "Cold ground was my bed last night, and rock was my pillow too," Marley sang to and of the sufferers in "Talkin' Blues."

Now fire glinted behind the window of the automobile as Marley lit a marijuana cigarette. He inhaled rapidly and deeply as the commissioner and his officers pretended that nothing out of the ordinary was taking place. For the first time that night, his taunt facial expression—the screwface—started to relax.

Then the line of cars slowed, and the screwface returned. This was not the National Heroes Circle Stadium. Here the fires burned brighter, and mobs of people flooded the street, surrounding the cars, rocking them, peering through the windows. Huge bonfires blazed, and amplified dance music crackled through tinny loudspeakers. This was, Marley immediately realized, the stronghold of the JLP. Somehow, the motorcade had blundered into a JLP "garrison" in the middle of an election rally.

DANGER AGAIN

"JLP War Zone" proclaimed the brightly colored letters on the neighborhood's cinderblock walls, and that was no exaggeration. The ghettos of Kingston were divided into many such garrisons, each of them claimed and controlled by gunmen loyal to the two rival political parties, the JLP and the PNP. In the ghettos, where most of Jamaica's voters lived, the parties fought for allegiance, buying loyalty with jobs, housing, and handouts, and enforcing it at the barrel of a gun. Party loyalty in Jamaica was almost akin to religious faith, and national elections were contested in an atmosphere just short of outright civil war. To back the wrong party could cost people their jobs, their houses, even their lives. The "ranking" gunmen of each party became celebrities in their own right, powerful figures revered as Robin Hoods by their followers, reviled as gangsters and terrorists by their opponents. The

1976 election campaign had already been the bloodiest in Jamaica's history.

The JLP faithful did not warmly receive the intrusion of a government motorcade into their garrison. They swarmed around the vehicles, undeterred by the sight of police uniforms or the sirens whirring on the vehicles' roofs, slowing the progress of the cars to a crawl and then a complete halt. They peered inside the windows, trying to see who had dared breech their stronghold.

Those inside the vehicles were not much happier. Was it a mistake that had brought them here or more "poli-tricks," as the sufferers called it, of the same kind that had gotten Marley and his wife and friends shot up in their home two nights earlier? The shootings had clearly been a setup of some kind, since the government guards appointed to patrol around the house strangely disappeared just before the gunmen burst in and began firing. Only Jah had allowed his prophet to survive. Was he now being delivered to his enemies, handed over for elimination, by his self-proclaimed friends in the PNP, whose integrity he had good cause to mistrust? Was the botched assassination now to be finished off properly?

Chanting campaign slogans, the crowd only seemed to grow larger and more agitated. What thoughts the screwface hid then are unknown, for in the dusk and firelight he was recognized. Beside him, the police commissioner went unnoticed, but there was no mistaking the identity of the man with the untamed lion's mane of dreadlocks, the wispy growth of beard on the chin and lower jaw, the light brown skin, the deep-set, dark, soulful eyes, the prideful carriage, and the indomitable air that seemed to proclaim, as he had once said about himself: "I don't come to bow. I come to conquer."

In an instant, the identity of the passenger spread through the crowd, his name whispered at first, like a curse or a blessing—in either circumstance something too sacred or powerful to be uttered aloud. It traveled to the outermost fringes of the crowd and then, like a wave gathering momentum, returned inward, gaining in power and volume as the onlookers, as if collectively obeying some unspoken order, parted to let the motorcade pass. As they did so, they called out his name, the solidarity of the sufferers, for this moment at least, overpowering the partisan call of poli-tricks.

"Bob Mar-ley! Bob Mar-ley! Bob Mar-ley!" they chanted over and over again, and the screwface dissolved into a gentle smile, then laughter.

The cheers of the crowd receded as the motorcade rolled onward, only to be replaced by a deeper roar, heard first through the crackling static on the walkie-talkie and then outside, all around them, filling the night. They were approaching the National Heroes Circle Stadium, and the huge throng there had just heard an official announcement from the stage: Bob Marley was not only alive but was just minutes away. He would, as originally promised, sing for the people that evening.

7

Dancing in the Spirit

Most of Bob Marley's band was still in hiding, and his wife, Rita, had just been released from the hospital and was waiting backstage, dressed in her hospital gown and bandages. Upon reaching the stadium, Marley was embraced by Michael Manley and surrounded by a protective circle of 200 musicians and friends, offering themselves as human shields in case snipers were hiding among the otherwise ecstatic crowd of 80,000 people. It took Marley several minutes to quiet the roar that the throng sent up when it heard the stage announcer proclaim: "The great, the great, the great, the great Bob Marley!"

"When me decided to do this here concert two-and-a-half months ago," Marley said, "me was told there was no politics." He shook his dreadlocks in disgust. "I just wanted to play for the love of the people." Explaining that he was unable, because of his wounds, to play the guitar, he said he would sing just one song. Then he let loose an unearthly,

Two days after he was shot in December 1976, Bob Marley performed in the Smile Jamaica concert at the National Heroes Circle Stadium in Kingston. At the beginning of the concert, he told the crowd of 80,000 that he would sing one song. Then he performed for the next 90 minutes.

reverberating wail, equal parts rebel cry and the screech of a jungle bird, that cued the pickup group of crack reggae musicians assembled onstage.

Shaking his mane of dreadlocks, bobbing up and down and dancing, feet together, in the movement he called the "rebel's hop," Marley brought his right hand to his temple and then extended it, forefinger first, toward his audience—a prophet's gesture, admonishing them to listen to what he had to say. Then he chanted as much as sang the opening words to a song from his most recent album, one that he had never played before an audience in his homeland. "What life has taught me," he sang, "I would like to share with those who want to learn."

He was "dancing in the spirit," said the I-Threes, who had long been convinced that when Marley was onstage he became entranced, virtually possessed. The backing vocalists regularly "saw spiritual things happen to Bob onstage that no one else was conscious of," Rita said. "Languages, Bob talking in tongues in his songs." He continued to chant as he spun around and around, dreadlocks whirling, his right forefinger pointing out to the audience, then up to the heavens, warning that "until the philosophy which holds one race superior and another inferior / is finally and permanently discredited and abandoned—everywhere is war, me say war." The song was "War," Marley's musical adaptation of a speech on human rights given by Haile Selassie.

There was no containing Marley in the circle of protectors now, and any idea he had held about limiting himself to one song was quickly forgotten. For 90 mesmerizing minutes he continued, singing his "songs of freedom." At the end, still in the spirit, he rolled his left sleeve up and unbuttoned his shirt, triumphantly displaying his bullet wounds to the crowd. "You can't kill Jah," he had earlier sung—nor his messenger either, he now demonstrated. He crouched and put his hands at his hips, mimicking a gunfighter about to unholster his pistols. Then he drew, in the "bang-bang" gesture seemingly and sadly familiar to children everywhere, threw back his dreadlocks, and laughed. It sounded, said one who was on stage, "like a lion's roar." The prophet left the stage, and the next morning, he left his own land.

EXODUS

If the gunmen and the authorities had thought they could silence Marley, they were mistaken. After relocating to London and Miami, where he settled his wife, his children, and his mother, he produced two albums that represented a reassessment, not retreat. *Exodus*, released in the summer of 1977, was Marley's biggest-selling album to date, remaining on the British charts for 56 weeks and yielding three smash singles—"Exodus," "Jammin'," and "Waiting in Vain," the last being one of Marley's finest love songs, written for Cindy Breakespeare. Other songs, like "Guiltiness," were clearly inspired by the assassination attempt. The title cut reflected Marley's growing interest in Africa, both as the homeland of his ancestors and the literal and figurative promised land of his religion.

A European tour followed the album's release, but plans for American shows were canceled after the big toe on Marley's right foot was spiked during a pickup soccer game in Paris. He continued with the European dates, but to his great annoyance, the wound grew extremely painful and refused to heal; at the end of a show, he often had to pour blood from his boot. A London doctor diagnosed the toe as cancerous and recommended amputation, but Marley refused and sought another opinion. Rasta tenets forbade such procedures, he explained.

"Rasta no abide amputation," he said. "I and I don't allow a man to be *dismantled*." A Miami physician suggested the less invasive procedure of a skin graft, to which Marley agreed.

The period of enforced rest that followed the procedure, spent mainly in Miami, inspired Marley's most reflective album, *Kaya* (another Jamaican word for marijuana), which was released in the spring of 1978. A series of lovely, lilting hymns to the simple joys of life—sunshine, a misty morning, being in love—the record yielded one of Marley's biggest hits,

"Is This Love?" Though some saw the album as a withdrawal from political concerns, Marley had always seen political struggle as the means to an end—the ability of individuals to live their life on Earth joyfully. He explained:

> You can't show aggression all the while. To make music is a life that I have to live. Sometimes you have to fight with music.... But me always militant, you know. Me too militant. That's why me did things like *Kaya*, to cool off the pace.... I know when everything is cool and I know when I tremble, do you understand? Because music is something that everyone follows, so it's a force, a terrible force.

A RETURN TO JAMAICA

Further proof of the forcefulness of Marley's music and presence came in February 1978, when he returned to Jamaica for the first time since the attempt on his life. In his absence, political violence in Jamaica had escalated to such an extreme that the ranking gunmen of the two opposition parties, Claudie Massop and Bucky Marshall, felt compelled to call upon the only man with the influence to bring about peace on the island: Bob Marley. When Marley's plane landed in Kingston on February 24, a huge crowd showered him with adoration, reminding many onlookers of Haile Selassie's dramatic visit 12 years earlier. Nearly two months later, Marley gave a riveting performance at the One Love One Peace concert, which reached a dramatic conclusion when Marley persuaded political enemies Michael Manley and Edward Seaga to join hands onstage and pledge themselves to peace in Jamaica. Rarely had the ability of music to affect positive change been so tangibly demonstrated.

As the One Love One Peace concert demonstrated, Marley was ready to return to the stage. The world tour that followed was a succession of artistic and personal triumphs, its magnificence well documented on the live album *Babylon by Bus*. In the United States, as elsewhere, Marley was now playing larger venues than ever. The review of his June 1978 performance at Madison Square Garden by John Rockwell of *The New York Times* could have described the entire tour: "The concert was a triumph, for reggae in general but for Mr. Marley in particular.... Mr. Marley was extraordinary. Who would have believed Madison Square Garden would have swayed *en masse* to a speech by Haile Selassie, the words of which Mr. Marley incorporates verbatim into 'War'?"

While in New York, Marley received one of his greatest honors. The combined African delegations to the United Nations presented the singer with the Third World Peace Medal "on

Bob Marley extends his fist as he sings during a concert in Stockholm, Sweden. A European tour followed the release of *Exodus* in 1977. Plans for an American tour, however, were canceled after cancer was discovered in Marley's toe.

Ziggy Marley and the Melody Makers

David "Ziggy" Marley, Bob and Rita Marley's oldest son, was named after the biblical king David, but he quickly acquired the name "Ziggy" from his father. It was a nickname the elder Marley also had as a youngster; he passed it on to his infant son just days after his birth. Ziggy was a name that meant that he had good legs for soccer, that he had the coordination to outrun everyone else on the field.

Ziggy was born in October 1968, at a time when his father was struggling to make money as a musician and the growing family—which included sisters Sharon and Cedella—still lived in one cramped bedroom in the home of Rita Marley's Aunt Viola. Ziggy Marley first went into his father's studio at the age of 10, and he was continually surrounded by the music of his father and other musicians of the era.

Throughout his childhood, it was apparent that Ziggy Marley, as well as his siblings, had great musical abilities. In 1979, the three oldest Marley children—joined by Rita and Bob's youngest son, Stephen—made their first track as Ziggy Marley and the Melody Makers, a name they borrowed from a British rock magazine called *Melody Maker*. Their first song, "Children Playing in the Streets," was written for them by their father.

The group's first album, *Play the Game Right,* was released in 1985, followed by *Hey World!* in 1986. The next album, *Conscious Party*, won a Grammy Award for best reggae recording after being released in 1988. Several other albums followed, including the Grammy winners *One Bright Day* in 1989 and *Fallen Is Babylon* in 1997. Members of the group have said that their music is different from their father's, although they don't hesitate to comment about humanity and the problems that people face in the world.

In 2003, Ziggy Marley produced his first solo album, *Dragonfly.* Although he said working solo had never been a goal, he found the experience invigorating. Today, as other Marley siblings and half-siblings step out on their own, Ziggy Marley—now a father himself—may be the leader of an entire new generation of Marley recordings.

behalf of five hundred million Africans" for his work for "equal rights and justice." Meeting the press afterward, Marley explained how his music served that cause: "When you fight revolution, you use guns.... Well, the music is the biggest gun, because it *save*. It no kill, right?" Earlier that year, he made his first visit to the fatherland, to Kenya and Ethiopia, where a relative of Selassie's gave him a ring with the figure of a lion on it, which had once belonged to the emperor.

After shows in Europe, Marley and the Wailers became the first reggae group to tour the Far East. In Japan, the group was stunned when the audience at each show sang along with every word of every song. Then in New Zealand, a delegation of Maoris, the island's native people, made a pilgrimage to Auckland to welcome Marley officially. At a traditional native ceremony of greeting, they awarded him a name that translates as "the Redeemer."

AFRICAN SOLIDARITY

Marley returned to the studio in the first months of 1979 to record the songs for *Survival*. The new album reflected his concern with African solidarity and independence. Marley was especially gratified to learn that one of its tracks, "Zimbabwe," was immediately adopted as the anthem of the black freedom fighters who were working to end decades of colonial and white rule in the former British colony of Rhodesia.

The following April, Marley was invited to play at the ceremonies marking the official independence of the new nation of Zimbabwe. He would perform amid the ruins of Great Zimbabwe, a huge stone palace occupied by the kings of Zimbabwe before their nation was dominated by Great Britain. Marley was so moved by the invitation that he paid the enormous expense of transporting his musicians and all their equipment to Zimbabwe. While he waiting to change flights at Nairobi, Kenya, a messenger boarded Marley's plane with the information that Prince Charles of Great Britain, also on his way to the ceremonies in Zimbabwe, was in a nearby plane and would like Marley to come speak with him. "The prince want for see me," responded Marley in the best spirit of black independence, "him have for come here to me." Though the actual ceremonies were chaotic, resulting in an interruption of Marley's performance, he nevertheless regarded the event as the greatest honor of his career.

In May 1980, the Wailers embarked on their most ambitious tour yet, the Tuff Gong Uprising world tour. In six weeks in Europe, they played before more than one million fans in 12 cities, making them the biggest concert attraction to that point in the continent's history. In Milan, Dublin, and London, the group performed outdoor shows before crowds of more than 100,000. The Milan show even outdrew a recent appearance by the pope.

The triumphant tour was marred only by the increasingly evident fatigue of its leader. Though Marley roused himself onstage night after night to give what many consider to be the most inspired performances of his career, offstage he was haggard, constantly exhausted, and more withdrawn than usual. Regularly accommodating to the press, as a way to spread the message of Rastafari and reggae music, he now often asked keyboardist Tyrone Downie to be his spokesman.

Most of those closest to Marley supposed that he was simply worn out, physically and emotionally, by the accumulated demands placed on him by family, friends, favor seekers, hangers-on, and his music. "He was just so pressured by people everywhere he went," Cindy Breakespeare recalled. "They were just drawn like moths to a flame, they couldn't stay away." Wailer Al Anderson was somewhat less charitable, describing the situation as "too many sharks on one piece of meat." The undeniable truth of such observations nonetheless failed to disclose the real cause of Marley's malaise.

MARLEY COLLAPSES

The American leg of the Tuff Gong Uprising tour began in September 1980. On September 21, the morning after he played the second of two scheduled shows at Madison Square Garden in New York, Marley went for a jog in Central Park with Alan Cole and some other friends. He had gone just a short distance, however, when he called out to Cole and col-lapsed, going into convulsions. Cole managed to get Marley back to his hotel, and physicians were consulted. The band went ahead to Pittsburgh, the site of the next concert two days later. The ignored cancer from Marley's toe had spread throughout his body; the musician had an inoperable brain tumor, and the doctors estimated that he would live for only two or three more weeks.

Marley proceeded to Pittsburgh, determined to play the next show. Band members vividly recall the immense sorrow of the sound check that day, when Marley sang over and over an early number called "Keep on Movin'," until its chorus of "Lord, I got to keep on moving" brought the I-Threes to tears and they asked him to stop. That night he and the band took the stage unannounced, Marley piercing the auditorium's darkness with his ululating rebel's trill. "Yeaaah!" he shouted. "Greetings in the name of His Imperial Majesty, Emperor Haile Selassie I, Jah, Rastafari, who liveth and reigneth in I and I I-tinually, ever faithful, ever sure." He then played an unfor-gettable set. Appropriately, "Redemption Song" was the last

IN HIS OWN WORDS...

In 1980, Bob Marley was working on the *Uprising* album when he wrote "Redemption Song." The music to the song was said to be spiritual rather than reggae, and Marley's words have been inspirational to many people:

Emancipate yourselves from mental slavery
None but ourselves can free our minds
Have no fear for atomic energy
'Cause none of them can stop the time
How long shall they kill our prophets
While we stand aside and look
Some say it's just a part of it
We've got to fulfill the book

song on the last album released during Marley's lifetime, *Uprising*. That night onstage he played and sang it alone, picking out the beautiful melody on his battered acoustic guitar. "Won't you help to sing," he asked, "these songs of freedom, 'cause all I ever had—redemption songs; all I ever had, redemption songs, these songs of freedom, songs of freedom."

Backstage, the Wailers and the I-Threes sobbed. Judy Mowatt said:

> Now I realize what he went through. Alone, because it had to be alone. We did not know how he was hurting. We did not know the pain he was going through. We did not know if he was afraid. We did not know if he was wondering if he could do the show or not. He didn't say anything to anybody.

Summoning the Wailers back to the stage for four more songs, Marley closed the concert, fittingly, with "Work," with its countdown of "five days to go ... four days to go ..." When the show was over, he walked to the edge of the stage and shook hands with members of the audience.

At that point, Bob Marley decided to seek treatment for the cancer that was ravaging his body. He went to Germany for treatment that met his religious beliefs. Even though his life lasted about six months longer than doctors originally thought when his cancer was diagnosed, in the spring of 1981, Marley's German doctor said he had done everything possible. Marley asked Rita, who had just returned to Jamaica after being in Germany, to meet him in Miami and to bring the children along. He wanted to say good-bye. In her 2004 autobiography, *My Life With Bob Marley: No Woman No Cry*, Rita Marley remembers that day. He told son Ziggy: "On your way up, please take me up; and on your way down, don't let me down." And, to son Stephen, he issued this simple reminder: "Money can't buy life."

On May 11, 1981, at the age of 36, as he had foreseen, Bob Marley died in Miami, Florida. In different places in Kingston, Marcia Griffiths and Judy Mowatt received the news of his death, they said, in the form of a lightning bolt and thunder crash, whose import they each immediately understood. Marley's funeral in Jamaica was attended by every important politician and dignitary in the country. More appropriately, an estimated one million people—virtually half the island's population—lined the roads in respect as his body was driven to its final resting place, a simple mausoleum next to the tiny shack where he grew up in Nine Mile.

Marley's greater political and spiritual message endures throughout the world as well. Even though the CIA considers the Rastafarians a political pressure group in Jamaica, those who practice the religion try to stay true to its original cause—to be a group focused on peace, love and unity.

8

The Legend Lives On

Just two weeks before his sixtieth birthday celebration, Bob Marley's hit song, "No Woman, No Cry," was among 20 tunes selected by the Grammy Hall of Fame for their historical significance. A song deeply reminiscent of the young Marley's days spent growing up in Trench Town, it put words to the oppression that had occurred and has remained a song that crosses political, cultural, and religious boundaries.

Unlike many musicians and artists whose lives and accomplishments seem to stagnate after their deaths, the legend of Bob Marley only continues to grow. He was a quiet, pensive youngster when he was growing up in Trench Town, and his mother has said that there seemed to be a uniqueness in the young boy—a boy of small stature who had a knack for Jamaican football as well as music. "I came to acknowledge him as someone who was so different," Rita Marley recalled in the book *Bob Marley: Songs of Freedom*. "It wasn't about just being great: it was about being really different. And at that same time being able to maintain a certain humility, which was taken for granted by most of his friends…"

It was barely a year after Marley's death, though, that legal battles began for his family. The two other members of the original Wailers—Peter Tosh and Bunny Livingston—first decided that they would take over the Tuff Gong label. In response, Rita Marley established RMM, for Rita Marley Music, which she also said could stand for Robert Marley Music. Then, for several years, many people tried to lay claims on the Marley estate. Although myriad legal battles followed, Rita Marley and Bob's 12 children still control Marley's music.

Today, his music is heard around the world in its original versions and in many reissues. *Entertainment Weekly* reported in 2005 that Marley's songs had sold 21.3 million copies since

Rita Marley sat with two of his sons at the state funeral for Bob Marley held on May 21, 1981, in Kingston, Jamaica. For years after Marley's death, several people tried to lay claims on his estate.

1991. In 2000, *Time* magazine named his song "One Love" the Song of the Century. At the same time, the magazine also named Marley's album *Exodus* as the Album of the Century.

The Marley family continues to release material created by Marley, while new cuts are made involving past releases. Back in 1976, Marley's song "Johnny Was" was written as a protest song about a mother whose son had been shot down in the street. In October 2005, parts of that song were meshed with a hit by the late rapper Notorious B.I.G. called "Suicidal Thoughts." Sean "Diddy" Combs produced the new piece, which was named "Hold Ya Head." Combs apparently thought the combination was an interesting one since Notorious B.I.G. was shot and killed in Los Angeles. Not only does Marley's music live on, it continues to take on new life.

THE FAMILY

Rita Marley said that Bob's last words to her were, "Forget crying, Rita! Just keep singing." And she has, issuing several releases since his death. Bob and Rita Marley had four children of their own, and he had adopted Sharon, whom Rita had before they were married.

Bob and Rita's oldest son, Ziggy, has developed a musical career of his own after singing for many years with his siblings— Sharon, Cedella and Stephen—in a Grammy Award-winning group called the Melody Makers. Stephen heads up the family's music-production company, called Ghetto Youths International. Cedella Marley runs another family business called Tuff Gong, and she started a clothing line inspired by her father's style. Some of Marley's other children, who include Rohan, Robbie, Karen, Julian, Ky-Mani, Damian, and Makeda, have musical careers of their own. Marley's last seven children were born to different women, a fact that admittedly hurt Rita Marley. "I didn't think I could disrupt his relationships, though sometimes the situation was painful and I couldn't understand what was going on," she wrote in her autobiography.

Rita Marley—with three of Bob Marley's sons (from left) Damian, Stephen, and Julian—paid tribute to Bob Marley at the MOBO Awards (Music of Black Origin) in September 2005 in London.

Despite his mistakes, Bob Marley seemed to see himself as a servant of his Rastafarian Jah, and he used his humility to do what he saw as his life's work—spreading peace and love among the people of his native Jamaica, Africa, and the rest of the world.

After his death, Rita Marley established the Bob Marley Foundation in Jamaica, which has given money and support to families, a children's hospital, and many other charitable organizations. Eventually, Rita's attention turned to Africa, and to the poverty and health crises there. "It's not just about being his wife," Rita Marley said in her book, "it's about being a person who is carrying on a legacy that means so much in the world." Marley's children who were involved in the Melody Makers also created a foundation, called URGE (Unlimited Resources Giving Enlightenment).

The family also found it important that there be physical reminders of Bob Marley's life. The home that Chris Blackwell sold Marley on Hope Road in Kingston became the Bob Marley Museum, which features historic artifacts of Marley's career, writings, photographs, news clippings, and ads as well as guided tours and videos of Marley's live performances.

FULL CIRCLE

Dusty, unpaved roads lead the way to Nine Mile, the town in St. Ann Parish, Jamaica, where Bob Marley was born and where his body was put to rest after his death. Nine Mile is

The Bob Marley Foundation

The Bob Marley Foundation was established in 1986 by his wife, Rita, and some of his children, five years after the legendary reggae musician's death. Health, education, and nutrition are the primary concerns of this nonprofit, charitable organization formed to provide support to people living in poverty, specifically in Jamaica and Africa. The organization continues its effort to empower individuals, groups, and entire countries to overcome the oppression imposed on them for many generations.

Several of Marley's family members stay directly involved with the foundation, including Rita, who is the foundation's chairwoman; his daughter Cedella, who is the director; and his son Ziggy, the international advisor. The foundation has become involved with programs in Jamaican and Ethiopian schools, offering grants for books, teacher training, and improvements to classroom facilities.

Another concern of the foundation is health. Africa is plagued with AIDS, a disease that has killed more than 17 million people there. The foundation also provides support to organizations that help cancer patients and those who suffer from high blood pressure, malaria, and other illnesses.

Providing children with a good breakfast before they begin their school day has also been a foundation project. The organization helps establish canteens where children can get food before their classes begin, and it connects with various organizations around the world that deal with the issues of hunger and poverty.

where Cedella Marley Booker, Marley's mother, lived when she gave birth to her son and for a few years beyond that, until she brought him to Kingston, where she had gone hoping to find a better life. The fertile soil here is what made Marley's grandfather known as the best farmer of the region. Later in his life, Nine Mile was a place the famed musician would visit to meditate for peace and clarity.

Three small buildings remain standing there, surrounded now by pink roses and ferns. When Cedella Marley Booker isn't in Florida, where she spends much of her time, she tends to return to Nine Mile, where she will greet visitors. Marley's favorite spot for meditation, Mount Zion Rock, is still on the property. Nearby is the mausoleum with its stained-glass windows, where Marley's remains are kept. Visitors are often found in the marble tomb, a room that contains Marley's brass coffin, a guitar, a soccer ball, a Bible, and other symbols of his life.

Near the end of his life, Marley sought out his form of God, in the Rastafarians' Jah, to help keep the humility and focus that he knew was required. Just before he became severely ill, he was talking of settling down in Jamaica, of building a recording studio of his own and a house big enough for all of his children. This final dream, though, never came true.

Bob Marley was a man whose musical fame emerged from the political and social turmoil that surrounded him. While in life he was a small, wiry man, in death he is a giant, not only in the music industry, but as a prophet in the words he sang as he preached for equality and unity among all races of the world. Today his legacy lives on in the charitable work and music created by his children, his wife, and his fans around the world.

Selected Discography

Catch a Fire (1972)

Burnin' (1973, reissued 2001)

Natty Dread (1974)

Live! (1975)

Rastaman Vibration (1976)

Exodus (1977)

Kaya (1978)

Babylon by Bus (1978)

Survival (1979)

Uprising (1980)

Confrontation (1983)

Legend (1984)

Rebel Music (1986)

Talkin' Blues (1991)

Songs of Freedom (1992)

Natural Mystic (1995)

Dreams of Freedom: Ambient Translations of Bob Marley (1997)

Chant Down Babylon (1999)

One Love: The Very Best of Bob Marley and the Wailers (2001)

Africa Unite (November 2005)

1945	Is born Nesta Robert Marley on February 6, in the parish of St. Ann, Jamaica
1959	Makes singing debut at a talent show; begins studying music with singer Joe Higgs
1961	Forms the Wailers with Bunny Livingston and Peter Tosh
1963	Auditions with the Wailers for producer Clement Dodd; the Wailers record "Simmer Down" with the Skatalites
1965	Songs by the Wailers occupy 5 of the top 10 slots on the Jamaican record charts; Marley begins a romance with singer Rita Anderson
1966	Marley and Anderson are married; Emperor Haile Selassie I of Ethiopia visits Jamaica; Marley and the Wailers convert to Rastafari; they establish Wail'N Soul'M record label
1967	Wail'N Soul'M label fails; Bob and Rita Marley return to Nine Mile
1969	Marley writes and records for singer Johnny Nash and again for producer Leslie Kong; begins collaboration with Lee "Scratch" Perry and Aston "Family Man" Barrett
1971	The Wailers establish the Tuff Gong production company; their first release, "Trench Town Rock," tops the Jamaican charts for five months; the Wailers sign a contract with Island Records in Great Britain
1972	Island releases the Wailers' *Catch a Fire*, the first true reggae album
1973	The Wailers tour Great Britain and the United States; record their second album, *Burnin'*; Livingston and Tosh leave the group

1976	Jamaican government bans four songs from Marley's *Rastaman Vibration* album; Marley is shot in an assassination attempt; performs at Smile Jamaica concert; leaves Jamaica to live in London and Miami
1977	*Exodus* is released and remains on British charts for 56 weeks; cancer is discovered in Marley's toe
1978	Marley returns to Jamaica and performs at the One Love One Peace concert; receives the Third World Peace Medal from the African delegations to the United Nations
1980	Attracts record crowds on the Tuff Gong Uprising world tour; collapses in New York; cancer has spread through his body; plays his last concert in Pittsburgh
1981	Dies on May 11 in Miami
1986	The Bob Marley Foundation is created; the Bob Marley Museum opens in Kingston at his former home at 56 Hope Road
1994	Marley is inducted into the Rock and Roll Hall of Fame
2005	"No Woman, No Cry" is selected for the Grammy Hall of Fame

Barrett, Leonard. *The Rastafarians: Sounds of Cultural Dissonance.* Boston: Beacon, 1988.

Boot, Adrian, and Chris Salewicz. *Bob Marley: Songs of Freedom.* New York: Viking Studio, 1995.

Davis, Stephen. *Bob Marley.* Rochester, VT: Schenkman, 1990.

Davis, Stephen, and Peter Simon. *Reggae Bloodlines: In Search of the Music and Culture of Jamaica.* New York: Da Capo, 1992.

Lazell, Barry. *Marley.* London: Hamlyn, 1994.

Marley, Rita. *My Life With Bob Marley: No Woman No Cry.* New York: Hyperion, 2004.

Talamon, Bruce, and Roger Steffens. *Bob Marley: Spirit Dancer.* New York: Norton, 1994.

Taylor, Don. *Marley and Me: The Real Bob Marley Story.* New York: Barricade Books, 1995.

White, Timothy. *Catch a Fire: The Life of Bob Marley.* New York: Henry Holt, 1992.

Whitney, Malika Lee, and Dermott Hussey. *Bob Marley: Reggae King of the World.* San Francisco: Pomegranate, 1994.

WEBSITES

The Bob Marley Foundation
www.bobmarleyfoundation.org

The History of Jamaican Music, 1959–1973
http://niceup.com/history/ja_music_59-73.html

The Official Bob Marley Website
www.bobmarley.com

The Rita Marley Foundation
www.ritamarleyfoundation.org

The Ultimate Bob Marley Fan Site
www.thirdfield.com

The Wailers
www.wailers.com

The Wailers News
www.iration.com/wailers/

Sherry Beck Paprocki is a freelance journalist and has written or contributed to six books for children, including *World Leaders: Vicente Fox* (Chelsea House, 2002); *Women of Achievement: Katie Couric* (Chelsea House, 2001); and *Women Who Win: Michelle Kwan* (Chelsea House, 2001). In addition, her bylines have appeared in *Pages* magazine, *Preservation* magazine, *The Chicago Tribune*, the *Cleveland Plain Dealer*, *The Philadelphia Inquirer*, the Los Angeles Times Syndicate, and many other publications. She is a graduate of the Ohio State University School of Journalism and lives near Columbus, Ohio, where she also serves as an adjunct faculty member of Otterbein College.